OVERWHELMING RESPONSE FOR

DYING: A BOOK OF COMFORT . . .

"I tell my audiences that if they can only buy one book this season, it should be DYING: A BOOK OF COMFORT. . . . This book will become the vehicle for instilling hope and understanding in those who seek our support. . . . It is the book to which I turn in my own moments of darkness."
—**Judith A. Skretny, Life Transitions Center, lecturer and educator for the American Academy of Bereavement**

"With this beautiful book, Pat McNees becomes our caregiver as we struggle with the mystery of life and death, and thoughtfully enables us to comfort others."
—**Father Paul Keenan, author of *Good News for Bad Days***

"For those who face the lonely reality of death, this book provides understanding and much-needed solace."
—**Claire Berman, author of**
Caring for Yourself While Caring for Your Aging Parents

"The subject of death is so rife with terror that it takes a calm and sure hand like Pat McNees's to soothe, help us understand, and, finally, rejoice in life. This is an important and very dear book."
—**Sherry Suib Cohen, author of**
Secrets of a Very Happy Marriage

"Pat McNees gently guides us as we reluctantly explore the far side of forever. . . . On January 1, the anniversary of my mother's birthday, I read the chapter on the death of a parent and did, indeed, find it comforting."
—**Lynne Lamberg, author of**
Bodyrhythms: Chronobiology and Peak Performance

"It is a wonderful book . . . a great gift book. . . . People need this sort of information."
—**Kathleen Braza, grief counselor and producer of the video *To Touch a Grieving Heart***

more . . .

"A fine collection that will be helpful for the ill, the dying, and the grieving, as well as their caregivers."
—**Dr. John D. Morgan, coordinator of the Centre for Education about Death and Bereavement at King's College, London, Ontario, Canada**

"This is an excellent book—thoughtfully compiled, well-organized, and very, very helpful to anyone who must deal with the emotional and spiritual issues of dying."
—**Joan Detz, author of *How to Write & Give a Speech* and *Can You Say a Few Words?***

"I found DYING: A BOOK OF COMFORT valuable and expanding. . . . [This book] invites you to notice the love and wonder that are hidden in the routine situations of life."
—**Clint Walker, psychologist**

"Through its expertly chosen material, DYING: A BOOK OF COMFORT informs, guides, and gently enables healthy grief and mourning. I recommend it heartily."
—**Therese A. Rando, Institute for the Study and Treatment of Loss, author of *How to Go On Living When Someone You Love Dies***

"The book's greatest gift for us was that it contained the perfect poem for my mother to read at the graveside for my father's unveiling . . . the words were so beautiful and so apt."
—**Robin Henig, author of *How a Woman Ages***

"It feels like my daily devotional."
—**Donna Mayo, linguistic anthropologist**

"A superb anthology of comfort. . . . I have shared selected readings with the bereaved, with warm reception."
—**Jeffrey Price, Aftercare/Bereavement Services**

"A superb book. . . . A classic."
—**Andrea Warren, author of *Orphan Train Rider***

Dying

A Book of Comfort

selected and edited by
Pat McNees

WARNER BOOKS

A Time Warner Company

WARNER BOOKS EDITION

Copyright © 1996 by Doubleday Direct, Inc.
All rights reserved.
Copyright information continued on page 325.

This Warner Books edition is published by arrangement with Doubleday Direct, Inc., Garden City, NY

Warner Books, Inc., 1271 Avenue of the Americas, New York, NY 10020

Visit our Web site at http://warnerbooks.com

 A Time Warner Company

Printed in the United States of America

First Warner Books Printing: August 1998

10 9 8 7 6 5 4 3 2 1

Library of Congress Cataloging-in-Publication Data

Dying : a book of comfort / selected and edited by Pat McNees. -- Warner Books ed.
      p.   cm.
    Originally published: Garden City, N.Y. : GuildAmerica, c1996.
    Includes indexes.
    ISBN 0-446-67400-1
      1. Terminally ill--Prayer-books and devotions--English.   2. Death--Religious aspects.   3. Consolation.   I. McNees, Pat.
BL625.9.L53D85   1998
242'.4--dc21   98-13933
                                                                  CIP

*For the hospice workers and volunteers
who make it possible for us to help each other die at home,
and for Miriam McNair Scott,
who showed her friends how to say good-bye.*

Acknowledgments

Many people suggested material to include in this volume, or told me where to look for what is especially helpful to people who are dying, or grieving, or helping the dying or bereaved. I appreciate the insights of Edwina Moldover and Catherine Bates of the Montgomery County, Maryland, hospice societies, and patient explanations of the grieving process and suggestions about what to include (and leave out) from grief counselor Kathleen Braza. I am especially thankful to the following people, who guided me to authors or material or who read and commented on early drafts of the material: Kathleen Braza, Allan Casson, Jean Eggenschwiler, Cynthia Harrison, Rebecca Hirsh, Bayla Kraft, Jerry Masinton, Donna Mayo, Kay Miller, Angela Peckenpaugh, Mary Jo Reiter, Bert Reiter, Marc Renard, Marilynne Rudick, Barbara Baer Solomon, Andrea Warren, and Carolyn Weathers (of Clothespin Fever Press).

In connection with the death of my own father, I deeply appreciate the loving attention of my Aunt Gene and Uncle Clint Whelchel, who, when my father begged not to die in a hospital, welcomed him and my mother into their home for the better part of two years, and me for several months. Dr. Byron T. Song walked us through the dying process with compassion and respect. Celia Kaplan, Margaret Montes, Frances Amerio and the other hospice workers from the Hospice of the East San Gabriel Valley in West Covina, California, opened my eyes to the incredible way hospices help families like ours manage a death in the home.

Barbara Greenman, my editor at GuildAmerica Books, has been more actively involved in the preparation of this book than any editor I have ever worked with, partly because a dear friend had just died and she knew that a book like this would have helped her. I greatly appreciate Arlene Friedman suggesting me as editor for this collection, and Rachel Simon and Eric Hafker for sharing the work of turning a concept into a book.

Finally, thanks to the many writers whose works are reprinted here. I've kept bibliographical information to a minimum not out of ingratitude but because I wanted to keep this collection from looking like a schoolbook. People who are dying or grieving want comfort, even insight, but are daunted by something that looks like work. Things look harder when you're dealing with a death; thinking often seems especially difficult. I've tried to make the book emotionally accessible to the people who could most benefit from it.

Pᴀᴛ McNᴇᴇs

Contents

BRINGING DEATH BACK HOME

When I was twelve, a girl fell from a fifteen-foot cliff and landed at my feet. We were both on a group outing; she was walking along the high path, and I along a stream at the bottom. Just before she fell, she shouted something down to the three of us who were walking along the stream. I shouted back, "I can't hear you." Moments later she landed at our feet unconscious, a trickle of blood coming from her nose. While my friend Judy administered what she knew of first aid, I ran back along the creek, screaming for help—relieved not to be left alone with an unconscious person whose life I could not save. The girl (whom I barely knew) died the next day. For years I believed she had died not only because I'd shouted "I can't hear you" but also because I didn't know first aid. In those days people didn't talk to young people about their feelings when things like this happened; they happened and you went on. Not until my twenties did I make any connection between my feelings of guilt about that death and my insomnia, which had begun early in my adolescence.

Many years later, I learned that my father had lung cancer and was expected to live two years at best. He and my mother moved in with my aunt and uncle in Los

Angeles, to be near a major hospital. A few months before my father's death, a cousin called to say that I should fly out immediately to intervene between my mother and everyone else. Dad wanted to die at home, not in a hospital, but Mom wanted him in a nursing home; she was afraid he would be too much for them to handle, and was angry about the situation.

Dad did die at home, and what made that possible was the hospice system, one of the best things ever to happen to this country. As a terminally ill cancer patient, Dad qualified for hospice care, which meant that several times a week a home-care nurse came to the house, checked his vital signs, sent someone to bathe him, and talked with all of us but was especially supportive of Dad (a fearful man) and Mom (who felt surrounded by enemies). The nurse refereed our fights (ostensibly about medication but actually about control), explained what was happening every step of the way, and told us what we could do about it.

With the support we got from the hospice staff, we were able to take care of my father, and I got to know him in a way I never would have otherwise. Although the emotional dynamics in that household were intense, in a strange way the three months I spent with my dying father and the rest of my family were a positive experience, both healing and transforming. I truly felt needed and knew when we put Dad in the ground that I had done everything I could possibly do to help him leave this life peacefully. Helping my dying father eased his death and changed my view of myself. I was no longer the twelve-year-old girl who would run away from dying.

Not everyone would welcome such a close encounter with death or even have the luxury of being able to spend so much time with a friend or family member who is dying, but in most parts of the country there are now many kinds of support services to help, either with care of the terminally ill or with the complex and painful process of working through the many feelings of bereavement afterward. Most important is simply to understand the process of dying.

First of all, had we known it at the time, we would have been more understanding of my mother's anger, and would have recognized, as Dad did, that anger was her way of expressing fear, including the fear of screwing up. We also would have known, the day Dad died, that he was probably going to die soon. I was standing by his bed that morning when he asked, "Who are those people?" He had been telling me about his hallucinations, and for some reason I joined him in this one, in a dialogue that almost comically reflected his personality and our relationship.

"They're waiting for the plane," I said (don't ask me why; I don't know).

"What plane?"

"The one to Hawaii." A few years earlier Dad had enjoyed a trip to Hawaii, and the family had often laughed about his eating the orchid they put on his airplane lunch tray, thinking it was a fancied-up radish.

"We're going to Hawaii?" he asked, interested. And, after a long pause: "Who's paying for this trip?"

"I am, Dad. You don't have to worry about it."

After another hour or so: "How long will we be gone?"

"Two weeks," I said, kicking myself later for the shortness of the trip.

Dad fell asleep, and I left his room and told the rest of the family about our conversation. Later, when my aunt walked past his bed, he asked her, "When's the plane leaving?"

"Four-thirty," she told him.

Dad worried about money, so late in the afternoon I tried to reassure him: "Dad, you really needn't be concerned about the money. I'm paying for the trip."

"That two-bit trip?" he said, and fell asleep. He died quietly a few hours later. Apparently he had a bigger trip in mind.

〽

Nobody teaches us how to die, or how to help someone die; nor how to grieve, or how best to help the grieving. My emphasis in collecting material for this anthology has been on the emotional, not the practical, aspects of death and grieving. I have looked for selections that offer meaningful insights and experiences, comforting words and stories, some guidance, much reassurance. One thing is for sure: Whatever we're experiencing, someone else has been there before us.

This is not a how-to book, but I have chosen selections around several basic themes: the intensity with which life is experienced by people who know they are dying (and those who help them die), what it is like (emotionally) to die, how to help someone die, how to say good-bye,

what to expect from grief, and how to console the bereaved. There are special sections on mourning the death
of a parent, the death of a child, a death by suicide, or a
violent, unexpected death. There are selections about
near-death experiences, about life after death, and about
life *and* death. There is a section of prayers from many
faiths, and selections suitable for reading at funerals and
memorial services are so marked in the index.

PAT MCNEES

Illness as Awakening

Do not act as if you had ten thousand years to throw away. Death stands at your elbow. Be good for something, while you live and it is in your power.

Marcus Aurelius

When you accept that you're going to die, you kid yourself a little less. Priorities change; you look at life differently. When you begin to reflect on death, you begin to live. It is part of the process of growing up.

Allegra Taylor,
Acquainted with the Night

By "coming to terms with life" I mean: the reality of death has become a definite part of my life; my life has, so to speak, been extended by death, by my looking death in the eye and accepting it, by accepting destruction as part of life and no longer wasting my energies on fear of death or the refusal to acknowledge its inevitability.

Etty Hillesum,
An Interrupted Life:
The Diaries of Etty Hillesum,
1941–43

In my happier days I used to remark on the aptitude of the saying, "When in life we are in the midst of death." I have since learnt that it's more apt to say, "When in death we are in the midst of life."

> A Belsen survivor
> quoted in *The Oxford Book
> of Death*

People who know that they are going to die have an edge. All of us realize that sooner or later we are going to die, but we don't know when. Even in times of war, devastation, flood, or earthquake—even in the face of certain death—we are still uncertain. There are miracles. We count on them.

But sometimes death *is* certain, and when it is, the dying have the edge—the knowledge of *when*. That knowledge changes them.

> Ted Menten,
> *Gentle Closings*

Illness is the night-side of life, a more onerous citizenship. Everyone who is born holds dual citizenship, in the kingdom of the well and in the kingdom of the sick.

> Susan Sontag

LIFE INTENSIFIED

In 1984 novelist Reynolds Price became crippled by spinal cancer, and he eventually was confined to a wheelchair. At best, doctors predicted paralysis, acute pain, and an early death. He lost four years to a largely unhelpful medical system, but confronting his own mortality and physical limits essentially transformed his experience of life. After ten years of prolific creativity, in 1994 Price published A Whole New Life, *a compelling account of his confrontation with catastrophic illness and skilled but uncompassionate doctors and his belated discovery of biofeedback as a technique for managing pain.*

The very fact of strict limitations soon had me tasting a fresh intensity of focus and pleasure in the strengths that were left me. I'll risk the claim that, from the time I left rehab, I've taken more pleasure than most adults ever come to know from my present eyesight, hearing and taste, from the stretches of my skin that still have feeling, and from my mind's new grip on patience—surely more pleasure than I'd known till now, and I've been a competent epicure. To be sure, for some three years after rehab, I'd still be seized more than once a day by the ravenous physical hunger to *stand,* to rise to my feet, unfold to my full height and look straight forward, not merely up. If you could have given me just one unimpeded stretch, a quarter hour to walk through my house and out to the trees, I'd have let you take my legs from the knee down as grisly compost for your houseplants or garden. But even that hunger has died away; and I live on now in my natural posture, the shape of the crooked

lightning bolt on the skintight jersey of one of my childhood heroes, Captain Marvel.

So *disaster* then, yes, for me for a while—great chunks of
four years. *Catastrophe* surely, a literally upended life with
all parts strewn and some of the most urgent parts lost
for good, within and without. But if I were called on to
value honestly my present life beside my past—the years
from 1933 till '84 against the years after—I'd have to say
that, despite an enjoyable fifty-year start, these recent
years since full catastrophe have gone still better. They've
brought more in and sent more out—more love and
care, more knowledge and patience, more work in less
time.

Reynolds Price,
A Whole New Life

If you knew that you were going to die tonight, or merely
that you would have to go away and never return, would
you, looking upon men and things for the last time, see
them in the same light that you have hitherto seen them?
Would you not love as you never yet have loved?

Maurice Maeterlinck

Remember, friends, as you pass by,
As you are now, so once was I,
As I am now, so you must be,
Prepare yourself to follow me.

> From a headstone in Ashby,
> Massachusetts,
> quoted by Stephen Levine

Do not seek death. Death will find you. But seek the road which makes death a fulfillment.

> Dag Hammarskjöld

If only we could live our life as if each moment were our last . . . we would connect with that essential part of ourselves that does not die. Ask yourself, is my life equipping me for my death? Because you become what you practice. What you are is what you have been. What you will be is what you are now.

> Chagdud Tulku Rinpoche

The nearer she came to death, the more, by some perversity of nature, did she enjoy living.

> Ellen Glasgow,
> *Barren Ground*

People say that what we're all seeking is a meaning for life. I don't think that's what we're really seeking. I think that what we're really seeking is an experience of being alive, so that our life experiences on the purely physical plane will have resonance within our innermost being and reality, so that we actually feel the rapture of being alive.

Joseph Campbell

INTOXICATED BY MY ILLNESS

Being ill and dying is largely, to a great degree, a matter of style. My intention is to show people who are ill—and we will all be ill someday—that it's not the end of their world as they know it, that they can go on being themselves, perhaps even more so than before. They can make a game, a career, even an art form of opposing their illness. There are so many interesting and therapeutic things they can do. It's not enough to be "positive," brave, or stoical: These are too simple, like New Year's resolutions. . . .

I would advise every sick person to evolve a style or develop a voice for his or her illness. In my own case I make fun of my illness. I disparage it. This wasn't a deliberate decision; the response simply came to me. Adopting a style for your illness is another way of meeting it on your own grounds, of making it a mere character in your narrative. . . . I think that only by insisting on your style can you keep from falling out of love with yourself as the illness attempts to diminish or disfigure

you. Sometimes your vanity is the only thing that's keeping you alive, and your style is the instrument of your
vanity. It may not be dying we fear so much, but the
diminished self. . . .

As a preparation for writing, as a first step toward
evolving a strategy for my illness, I've begun to take tap-
dancing lessons, something I've always wanted to do.
One of my favorite examples of a patient's strategy
comes from a man I know who also has prostate cancer:
Instead of imagining his good cells attacking his bad cells,
he goes to Europe from time to time and imposes Conti-
nental images on his bad cells. He reminds me that in an
earlier, more holistic age, doctors used to advise sick
people to go abroad for their health. . . .

A critical illness is like a great permission, an authori-
zation or absolving. It's all right for a threatened man to
be romantic, even crazy, if he feels like it. All your life
you think you have to hold back your craziness, but when
you're sick you can let it out in all its garish colors.

. . . I realized for the first time that I don't have
forever. Time was no longer innocuous, nothing was casual anymore. I understood that living itself had a dead-
line—like the book I had been working on. How sheepish
I would feel if I couldn't finish it. I had promised it to
myself and to my friends. Though I wouldn't say this out
loud, I had promised it to the world. All writers privately
think this way. . . . While I've always had trouble con-
centrating, I now feel as concentrated as a diamond or a
microchip.

Sartre was right: You have to live each moment as if you're prepared to die.

Anatole Broyard,
Intoxicated by My Illness

We cannot influence death but we can influence the style of our departure. Men surprise themselves by the fashion in which they face this death: some more proudly and more valiantly than ever they dared imagine; and some in abject terror.

Cyrus L. Sulzberger,
My Brother Death

BEING ALIVE

I'm having trouble dealing with those around me who ask in shrewd and subtle ways, "Why bother?"

People are criticizing me for my health foods and the way I'm caring for myself. Some laughed when I went through the Total Health Clinic. Yet the result of that analysis showed me how to put my body back into functional use again.

When I went I knew those critics were saying, "she's going to die anyway," and that's true. I am, but what I learned there is helping me with the dying because it has improved the quality of the life I have left. The vitamins and diet prescribed by the clinic make me feel better. I know they won't cure my cancer, but I am functioning better physically, mentally and spiritually, and whether it's for a day, or a week, or a year, that's worthwhile to me because I've still got some things to do before I die.

Perhaps the most important task remaining is to teach my husband how to deal with the I.R.S. I've taught him how to cook, and he's doing very well, thank you. He can even make yogurt. Furthermore, he's learned to shop for groceries, do the laundry, and sew on buttons. But he still needs to learn how to keep his own records for tax purposes, as well as know how to decipher the old ones I prepared since I can't leave a phone number behind.

I'm looking at death as my last journey and, obviously, I've already started that trip. On the way to my destination I want to be able to laugh with my husband as we do these parting things together, and I want to enjoy every minute I've got left.

Why bother? Why not, if it adds to the quality of my lifestyle and my last journey.

Thank you, dear God, for the help that makes me feel better.

> Ann Johnson,
> in *Meditations for the Terminally Ill and Their Families*

People who know they are going to die spend their remaining time either a) being alive; or b) staying alive.

The people who fit into the first category enjoy the time they have left. Those who concentrate on staying alive, however, spend every waking moment looking for a cure, running from doctor to doctor, drug to drug, hope to hope.

For people with AIDS, the desire to stay alive is urgent as they scramble for treatments to delay their deaths, knowing that a cure may be years away.

It's natural to want to survive. But often the frantic search for a wonder drug or a miracle cure only speeds the progress of the disease instead of retarding it. And all too often the process of staying alive destroys the process of being alive.

Again and again I have watched weeks of searching turn into months of searching, until the few remaining years dwindle away without any joy or happiness.

Ted Menten,
Gentle Closings

One must wait until the evening to see how splendid the day was; one cannot judge life without *death*.

George Bernard Shaw

The acknowledgement of impermanence holds within it the key to life itself. . . . In reality, all the time we have is right now. The past and the future are dreams. Only this moment is real. If we come newborn to each moment, we will experience life directly, not dream it.

Stephen Levine

The butterfly counts not months, but moments, and has time enough.

Rabindranath Tagore

HELPING

THE DYING

There is no cure for birth and death save to enjoy the interval. The dark background which death supplies brings out the tender colors of life in all their purity.

George Santayana

A friend is a present you give yourself.

Robert Louis Stevenson

HELPING A FRIEND

My friend Jenny needed me sometimes in the middle of the night when she couldn't sleep. She was dying of a cancer that consumed her body like a fast-burning brush fire, and toward the end even pain killers and sleeping pills didn't help. We had signals worked out between us: she would dial my number and let the phone ring only once so as not to waken Jack. It was spring then, too. I'd throw on a rain coat over my thin cotton nightgown and go out the back door and through the neighbors' yards to her house on the next street. . . .

I had my own key and even knew the stairway well enough to avoid the third and seventh treads, the ones that might waken others who surely needed their sleep. I can't tell you what a gift it was for me to be called upon that way. I never felt more alive than in those few months Jenny let me help her die.

I came at her call one night bringing a little basket of polish and implements to do her nails. She lay curled on the edge of a king-sized bed filled with pillows of every size. . . .

This was still a feminine room despite white enamel basins and collections of pills and capsules in child-proof caps; the woman in the bed steadfastly insisting on remaining a woman, not merely a patient. Her bright blue and green flowered nightgown slipped from shoulders where the flesh now stretched taut as canvas prepared for a painting. Her eyes were closed when I tiptoed in, trying to compose myself, trying to think of something to say that would not be trivialized by her drama. "How was your day? What's new?" Even the talk we call "small" seemed bathed in irony.

"I feel just awful," she said without opening her eyes. "Sit here on the bed next to me. Don't talk. Just hold my hand." Her pulse threaded under my palm. "What can I do for you?" I said at last, and when she didn't answer I picked up a heavy wooden hairbrush and smoothed her hair. Over and over I pulled the bristles through the still-gleaming black strands. "Such beautiful hair," I crooned, petting her, caressing the wasted arms, the bent shoulders, the submissive back.

I said, "Look what I've brought you," and spread the little bottles and tools on a nearby table. One by one, I filed her waxy-colored nails into almond shapes, chose from the assortment the sauciest red I could find, and made of each nail a defiant flag. "Don't move," I said as if she had somewhere to go. She spread her fingers on the coverlet, her gypsy coloring, always so vivid, almost garish now that her cheeks glowed faintly yellow under her tanned skin.

✨

Ours was a recent friendship though I had known about her for years: an artist, what I would call a patrician, with her impeccable WASP credentials, her prominent husband—just the kind of person whose acquaintance my reverse snobbery would keep me from pursuing. Merely comparing her upbringing to mine made me feel like someone just out of steerage, a bundle in one hand, a squawking chicken in the other.

But we did meet, at the home of a neighbor who knew us both, and in fifteen minutes over coffee Jenny and I discovered correspondences only women in their late forties will admit to; by the time we agreed to lunch the next day on egg salad sandwiches at the People's on Wisconsin, we were anticipating the kind of deep new friendship each of us had stopped expecting long before. For about two years after that, we saw each other almost every day, commiserated about our teenagers, laughed about the gray in our hair (the dread badge of courage) but refused to cover it, took classes together at G.W. and drank coffee in the student union, talking politics and gossiping about favorite professors with classmates half our age. . . .

☀

I was in my kitchen the morning Jenny called me from the doctor's office: "It's cancer," she said, almost in amazement, "the galloping kind. There's no hope, darling." I held my breath, and the protective shutters slammed down like those formidable barricades in front of little shops in France. What did that mean, "no hope"? Who said the word "cancer" out loud? What kind of doctor told patients they had nothing to pray for? This was the gentile world with a vengeance: stiff upper lip where my people would have rent their clothing, howled about the injustice—and consulted another doctor. But secretly I shuddered with a kind of relief. Lightning doesn't strike in the same place twice. Perhaps my own body would be safe for a little while. We talked second opinions; I hung up the phone and wept.

"There's one more thing you can do for me," Jenny said, cupping her fingers so she could blow her nails dry. "I'm dying for a shower." She rolled her eyes. "Joke," she said, and then, "Do you think you could help me?" She drew her legs up and pulled herself to a sitting position, biting her lower lip until it was pale between her teeth. Outside, on Newark Street, an automobile passed, radio blaring. "Please," she said. "Sponge baths just won't do it. I would feel so much better if I could only get under the water."

She saw my reluctance. Did I really want this responsibility? What if she stumbled, or fainted in the tub? For a moment I was struck by an absurd shyness; our 2:00 A.M. assignations seemed suddenly juvenile to me, something kids might do, not two grown women, one of whom was dying. Jenny pushed the blankets behind her. "You can't hurt me, you know. I'm past all that."

I put my arms around her waist and held her in front of me while we inched forward to the hallway, stopping every few feet for her to catch her breath. Each flaw in the polished wood floor, even the metal strip that anchored the hall carpeting, presented an obstacle. By the time we reached the bathroom, we were both sweating. While I steadied her, Jenny reached down, gathered up the silk hem of her gown, and drew it over her head.

It was clear I needed to turn my face from her as much to preserve my own privacy as hers, but Jenny was too close to me in that small room, her nakedness palpable, something I couldn't avoid, no matter where I looked. If Jenny noticed my hesitation, she didn't acknowledge it. "Quick," she said, hugging her elbows, swaying. "Help me!"

I sat her down on the closed toilet seat and adjusted the faucets so the shower ran a gentle blood warm. Then, taking her under the armpits, I half lifted, half dragged her into the tub. When she was standing under the spray, I pulled the plastic curtain over my body between us, partly to shield myself from some of the water, and partly because it was one more way to define myself as separate from her, another way of saying that when all this was over, I could walk away from her dying.

"Are you okay?" I kept saying. Steam fogged the window and the mirror and beaded the toilet and sink. Water ran down the arm with which I held Jenny and began to soak my cotton gown. "This is heaven," she said, lifting her face to the stream. "I wish I could stand here forever." And I thought, these are the elements to which we are finally reduced. After the refusal to believe, after the wrenching leave-takings and the resignation, come the small gifts freshly seen. Days before, I had cooked young carrots, no bigger than a thumb, and brought them to her in a pale blue bowl. We both cried when she licked the crumbs: another spring, all she was leaving—a smear of buttery sweetness on her fingers.

No way to stay dry, and I hadn't the heart to call an end to the bathing just yet. On an impulse, I stripped off my dripping gown and stepped into the tub with her. As she leaned her back into my body, I shampooed her thick hair with sweet-smelling soap and let the water plaster the strands against her head. I soaped her neck and shoulders, down her arms and then the backs of her legs, which had begun to tremble from fatigue under my hands.

Later we sat drinking tea in her room, our heads wrapped turban-style in white terry towels, Jenny back in bed and I, wearing one of her robes, in a chair nearby. She was exhausted, her bit of hoarded energy expended, spilled like sugar from a cloth sack. I said, "Jenny, I'm sorry. I shouldn't have let you do this. You'll be a wreck today." But all the while I kept thinking of my father, on his deathbed, refused the cigarette that had become his final shamefaced request. "They're bad for you, Daddy," I had told him, still pretending at the very end. I wish now I had given him that smoke, what difference would it have made to anyone but him?

When Jenny's hair was dry, she lay back against the

pillows, as if asleep. The room was so quiet I could hear someone in another part of the house murmur in a dream. Through trees in full leaf, the sky, starless, appeared as patches of blue enamel. "I never knew it would be so hard," Jenny said, turning her head to me, eyes still closed. "Hard to die, you mean?" She opened her eyes for a moment and looked straight at me. "Hard to keep on living," she said.

Faye Moskowitz,
And the Bridge Is Love

The world feels dusty
When we stop to die;
We want the dew then,
Honors taste dry.

Flags vex a dying face,
But the least fan
Stirred by a friend's hand
Cools like rain.

Mine be thy ministry
When the thirst comes,
Dews of thyself to fetch
And holy balms.

Emily Dickinson

There is a land of the living and a land of the dead and the bridge is love, the only survival, the only meaning.

> Thornton Wilder,
> *The Bridge of San Luis Rey*

When my father died, I tried to write a novel about it, but I found that my whole novel was written politely. I was so pious about death that it was intolerable, and I find that people are doing that to me now. They're treating me with such circumspection. They're being so nice to me. I don't know whether they really mean what they say or whether they're accommodating me. It's as though they're talking to a child, and I want them to stop that. I can't find them anymore. I need their help, but not in this form.

> Anatole Broyard,
> *Intoxicated by My Illness*

She enjoyed working with dying patients. There was something terribly *real* about many people when they got close to death, as if they no longer had the time to waste being inauthentic.

> M. Scott Peck,
> *A Bed by the Window*

HELPING SOMEONE DIE
WITH DIGNITY

As we have learned over the years, all people are the same, and their gratitude is the same if they can only find one human being who takes an hour out of a busy schedule to sit with them and help them to die with dignity— that means to die in character and not be put into our own mold, gratifying our own needs under the pretext that we are serving them, when in fact we impose our own needs onto them.

All the patients, each in his or her own way, have expressed their own needs, their own wishes, and we have tried to gratify them. There are some who desperately need denial of their illness, but this is a small percentage of the population, only one percent. Our greatest service to them is to accept this need, to allow them their denial without making them feel guilty or unworthy or labeling them, consciously or unconsciously, with "a lack of courage." They have used denial all their life, and they want to use it in the final phase of their life as well. For them, to die with dignity means to keep that denial, never shed a tear in public, and we allow them, naturally, to live up to their own expectations and needs. This has to be their own choice.

Others will fight to the very end. They are the fighters and the rebels, often of the new generation. They are enraged that they have just started to live and their life is ended before they have experienced a first love, a marriage, maybe a child, before they have fulfilled their professional dreams, before they have truly lived. And it is important that we do not sedate these patients, that we allow them to ventilate and externalize their rage, their anger, and their need to try every possible medical and sometimes not "socially acceptable" treatment so that they are able to say, "I have had everything possible that is available on the market," whether this is Food and Drug Administration approved or not. It is not up to us to tell people what they are allowed to try when their own life is at stake.

There are others who bargain with God till the very end. And it has to be understood that the promises that they make to God are practically never kept. A young mother who prays that she can live long enough to see her children out of school will add a quick prayer that she can stay alive until her children get married, and on the day of the wedding she will add yet another prayer that she will live long enough to become a grandmother. For us this is the most normal human behavior. We would never challenge these promises, in spite of the fact that we know they will only be replaced by more promises later on. It is important that at all times we be in touch with our own feelings and our own projections, so that we can help and serve the patient and not our own needs.

Anyone who has witnessed a patient in peace and not in resignation will never forget it and will have no problem differentiating between an old man in despair who wants to die because the quality of his life is such that it is not worth living, and an old man who had found peace and acceptance because he has been able to look back at his life and say, "I have truly lived."

Elisabeth Kübler-Ross,
To Live Until We Say Good-Bye

A dignified, or "good," death is one in which there is no railing or struggling against imminent death—above all, a death without sadness, without regret, without apprehension, without bitterness, without terror. It is dying freely, naturally, like falling asleep, not clinging to or clutching at life, just "going with the flow"—not "flow" or "letting go" in a psychological sense, but in the transcendent sense of the "eternal yea," of yielding to an inner, mysterious force that takes over when all self-striving ceases.

Philip Kapleau

LEAVING THE GOOD LIFE

Scott and I were winding up our lives together and we knew it. There were the physiological factors to be considered: how did he want to be treated, where, and by whom. I knew he desired to stay at home, not in a hospital with lifesaving apparatus all around. He would take no pills, no drugs, and hoped to avoid doctors. He had become less and less concerned with continuing to inhabit a weakening body. When he could no longer carry his part of the load and take care of himself, he was ready to go on. I was at one with him in this. The way one dies, it seemed to me, should reflect the way one had lived, and I was glad to help him do it gracefully. . . .

Scott had long talked of a purposeful and deliberate death. He was not going to wait until he was totally incapacitated and had become a burden to himself and others. He did not want to go through the horrors of a long decay in a nursing home.

"Why do we make such a hullaballoo of our last days and of dying?" he queried. Instead of quiet harmonious fading away in congenial familiar surroundings, we ship our loved ones to hospitals or nursing homes where, at great expense, they are maintained by strangers who try to stave off death by artificial means instead of easing and abetting the process. We enter with discomfort and a cry, but we can depart in dignity and completion, having fulfilled at least in part our purpose. . . .

A month and a half before Scott went, a month before his hundredth birthday, while sitting with a group at the table one day, he said: "I think I won't eat any more." He never took solid food again. He deliberately and purposefully chose the time and the way of his leaving. It was to be methodical and conscious. He would cast off his body by fasting.

Death by fasting is not a violent form of suicide: it is a slow gentle diminution of energies, a peaceful way to leave, voluntarily. Externally and internally he was prepared. He had always liked Robert Louis Stevenson's "Glad did I live and gladly die, and I lay me down with a will." Now he could put this into practice. He himself inaugurated his own technique for dying: let the body itself give up its life.

I acquiesced, realizing how animals often leave life—creeping away out of sight and denying themselves food. For a month I fed Scott just on juices when he wanted any liquids: apple, orange, banana, grape, whatever he could swallow. Then he said: "I would like only water." Yet he did not sicken. He was still lucid and spoke with me, but his body was extremely emaciated. The life force in him was lessening.

A week more on water, and he was completely detached from life, ready to slip easily into that good night. His body had dried up; now it was withering away, and he could tranquilly and peacefully retire from it. I was with him on his couch and quietly urged him on, the morning of August 24, 1983.

Half aloud, I intoned an old Native American chant: "Walk tall as the trees; live strong as the mountains; be gentle as the spring winds; keep the warmth of summer in your heart, and the Great Spirit will always be with you."

. . . Slowly, gradually, he detached himself, breathing less and less, fainter and fainter; then he was off and free, like a dry leaf from the tree, floating down and away. "All . . . right," he breathed, seeming to testify to the all-rightness of everything, and was gone. I felt the visible pass into the invisible. . . .

Scott lived the good life and died the good death. He had lived fully at every moment and he died serenely. He went as he had wished—at home, without medications, doctors, or hospital confinement, and with Helen beside him. She had a joyous feeling that he had done well. Leonardo da Vinci wrote in 1500: "As a well-spent day brings happy sleep, so life well-used brings happy death."

There was no disturbance: he did not gasp or jerk or tremble. He just breathed softly until there was no breath left and he was no longer in the body. It was simple as could be. It was an easy passing and a beautiful one, just breathing life away. . . .

Scott's dying showed me the good way, the good death—a negation of pain and distress, with the currents of life still flowing on. For such there is no grief. In the loss of something there was the gain of something else: a glimpse of hope in this reposeful, purposeful ending.

> Helen Nearing,
> *Loving and Leaving the Good Life*

A good death does honor to a whole life.

> Petrarch

We are spirits. That bodies should be lent us while they afford us pleasure, assist us in acquiring knowledge, or in doing good to our fellow creatures, is a kind of benevolent act of God. When they become unfit for these purposes, and afford us pain instead of pleasure, instead of an aid become an encumbrance, and answer none of these intentions for which they were given, it is equally kind and benevolent that a way is provided by which we get rid of them. Death is that way.

Benjamin Franklin

The Silence that Goes Beyond Words

There is a time in a patient's life when the pain ceases to be, when the mind slips off into a dreamless state, when the need for food becomes minimal and the awareness of the environment all but disappears into darkness.

Those who have the strength and the love to sit with a dying patient in the *silence that goes beyond words* will know that this moment is neither frightening nor painful, but a peaceful cessation of the functioning of the body. Watching a peaceful death of a human being reminds us of a falling star; one of a million lights in a vast sky that flares up for a brief moment only to disappear into the endless night forever.

Elisabeth Kübler-Ross,
On Death and Dying

At the last, tenderly,
From the walls of the powerful fortress'd house,
From the clasp of the knitted locks, from the keep of
the well-closed doors,
Let me be wafted.

Let me glide noiselessly forth;
With the key of softness unlock the locks—with a
    whisper,
Set ope the doors O soul.

Tenderly—be not impatient,
(Strong is your hold O mortal flesh,
Strong is your hold O love.)

Walt Whitman,
"The Last Invocation"

CONTEMPORARY SOCIETY'S DISCOMFORT WITH DEATH

Death had replaced sex as the great unmentionable, to be denied in prospect, endured in a decent privacy, preferably behind the drawn curtains of a hospital bed, and followed by discreet, embarrassed, uncomforted mourning.

P. D. James

When a person is born, we rejoice, and when they're married we jubilate, but when they die we try to pretend nothing has happened.

Margaret Mead

No one came to see us. No one, except for the UPS man when Jules sent me books from the office, and manuscripts, too, so I wouldn't lose my editing touch. I stacked them in the corner of my bedroom and continued with *Anna Karenina,* even though I knew very well how it ended. I felt as though I had an obligation to go on until the train thundered out of the station.

Sometimes, when I went out to buy groceries or some books or a bouquet of daisies, because such things gave my mother pleasure out of all proportion to the act, I would run into some old friend . . . and I could almost see the sentence forming in their minds before they said it: "I've been meaning to stop by, but . . ."

Another small spark of anger would flare in my chest, then die through lack of oxygen, except for the afternoon when I went into the bookstore to buy a magnifying glass. Teresa said she thought it was the medication affecting my mother's vision. But I think it was just one more part of her too tired to go on.

When Mrs. Duane began to say she'd been meaning to stop by, I looked into her clear blue eyes, the color of sky, wise and so aware of the duplicity of what she was saying that they darted away from my own, and without thinking I interrupted, "Then do it. Don't tell me about it. Don't regret that you didn't. What she has is not catching."

"Ellen—"

"Don't," I said, my voice getting higher and louder. I realized that people in the store had stopped to listen but I didn't care. "No one has come to see my mother since the week before Christmas. She's lonely and she's sad and she thinks that everyone's forgotten her, and all because it's too uncomfortable for anyone to deal with anything deeper than winter ski plans and shopping for dinner." And I picked up my packages and left without paying. . . .

The next day Mrs. Duane called and asked if she could come over for lunch. I fixed chicken sandwiches and she and my mother ate at a properly laid table in the dining room—"placemats, Ellen," my mother had said. Mrs. Duane scarcely met my eyes. She gossiped with my mother about whose children were doing what and the January slump on Main Street.

> Anna Quindlen,
> in *One True Thing,* a novel
> about a mother's death from
> cancer

When the Doctor's Agenda Is Not Enough

The classic deathbed scene—in which the dying person ties up all emotional loose ends and imparts final wisdom to loved ones—is a myth, says Yale surgeon Sherwin Nuland in a beautifully written book called How We Die. *Many more people die in hospitals than ever before and few of us actually witness the deaths of those we love, says Nuland. Not only should our expectations be more realistic, but we should not trust so blindly in the recommendations of doctors, whose agendas are often quite different from those of their patients. Doctors' clinical opinions about surgery and treatments for patients with little chance of survival should be only one factor in what is surely a moral, personal, social, and spiritual decision. When Nuland's brother was dying of cancer, Nuland—believing that "hope" meant cure and rescue—recommended a series of chemotherapy treatments that had little chance of curing him. "What I succeeded in doing was to take away an opportunity for some months of being with his family, at peace, slowly dying of this disease. And what I exchanged for it was a death that was terribly, terribly difficult." In* How We Die *he clearly describes the major causes and likely courses of death in their clinical and biological reality, to reduce the likelihood that others will make similar painfully wrong decisions.*

We live today in the era not of the art of dying, but of the art of saving life, and the dilemmas in that art are multitudinous. As recently as half a century ago, that other great art, the art of medicine, still prided itself on its ability to manage the process of death, making it as tranquil as professional kindness could. Except in the too-few programs such as hospice, that part of the art is now mostly lost, replaced by the brilliance of rescue and, unfortunately, the all-too-common abandonment when rescue proves impossible.

. . . Too often, physicians misunderstand the ingredients of hope, thinking it refers only to cure or remission. They feel it necessary to transmit to a cancer-ridden patient, by inference if not by actual statement, the erroneous message that it is still possible to attain months or years of symptom-free life. When an otherwise totally honest and beneficent physician is asked why he does this,

his answer is likely to be some variation of, "Because I didn't want to take away his only hope." This is done with the best of intentions, but the hell whose access road is paved with those good intentions becomes too often the hell of suffering through which a misled person must pass before he succumbs to inevitable death. . . .

The lesson in all of this is well known. Hope lies not only in an expectation of cure or even of the remission of present distress. For dying patients, the hope of cure will always be shown to be ultimately false, and even the hope of relief too often turns to ashes. When my time comes, I will seek hope in the knowledge that insofar as possible I will not be allowed to suffer or be subjected to needless attempts to maintain life; I will seek it in the certainty that I will not be abandoned to die alone; I am seeking it now, in the way I try to live my life, so that those who value what I am will have profited by my time on earth and be left with comforting recollections of what we have meant to one another.

There are those who will find hope in faith and their belief in an afterlife; some will look forward to the moment a milestone is reached or a deed is accomplished; there are even some whose hope is centered on maintaining the kind of control that will permit them the means to decide the moment of their death, or actually to make their own quietus unhindered. Whatever form it may take, each of us must find hope in his or her own way. . . .

This hope, the assurance that there will be no unreasonable efforts, is an affirmation that the dignity to be sought in death is the appreciation by others of what one has been in life. It is a dignity that proceeds from a life well lived and from the acceptance of one's own death as a necessary process of nature that permits our species to continue in the form of our own children and the children of others. It is also the recognition that the *real* event taking place at the end of our life is our death, not the attempts to prevent it. We have somehow been so taken up with the wonders of modern science that our society puts the emphasis in the wrong place. It is the dying that is the important thing—the central player in the drama is the dying man: the dashing leader of that bustling squad of his would-be rescuers is only a spectator, and a groundling at that.

> Sherwin Nuland,
> *How We Die*

MY DOCTOR SHOULD KNOW BETTER

You don't really know that you're ill until the doctor tells you so. When he tells you you're ill, this is not the same as giving you permission to be ill. You eke out your illness. You'll always be an amateur in your illness. Only you will love it. The knowledge that you're ill is one of the momentous experiences in life. You expect that you're going to go on forever, that you're immortal. Freud said that every man is convinced of his own immortality. I certainly was. I had dawdled through life up to that point, and when the doctor told me I was ill it was like an immense electric shock. I felt galvanized. I was a new person. All of my old trivial selves fell away, and I was reduced to essence. I began to look around me with new eyes, and the first thing I looked at was my doctor.

. . . I would like a doctor who is not only a talented physician, but a bit of a metaphysician, too. Someone who can treat body and soul. There's a physical self who's ill, and there's a metaphysical self who's ill. When you die, your philosophy dies along with you. So I want a metaphysical man to keep me company. To get to my body, my doctor has to get to my character. He has to go through my soul. He doesn't only have to go through my anus. That's the back door to my personality.

I would hope that my doctor's authority and his charisma might help to protect me against what the anthropologist Richard Shweder calls "soul loss," a sense of terrible emptiness, a feeling that your soul has abandoned your ailing body like rats deserting a sinking ship. When your soul leaves, the illness rushes in. I used to get restless when people talked about soul, but now I know better. Soul is the part of you that you summon up in emergencies.

. . . My friends flatter me by calling my performance courageous or gallant, but my doctor should know better. He should be able to imagine the aloneness of the critically ill, a solitude as haunting as a Chirico painting. I want him to be my Virgil, leading me through my purgatory or inferno, pointing out the sights as we go.

Anatole Broyard,
Intoxicated by My Illness

After nearly a decade of working within the limitations of existing hospital programs I began to feel the strain of bucking the system. As long as I delivered my bears [stuffed animals, for terminally ill patients, especially children], told my . . . stories and didn't get in anyone's way, I was welcome in almost any hospital across the country. But if I advised a family to take their loved one home to die, I was "out of line." If I suggested that a hospice might be a more loving environment than a hospital, I was "out of line." If I encouraged a patient to make a living will to prevent being hooked up to machines, I was "out of line." And if I suggested that patients have a right to die on their own terms, I was definitely "way out of line."

Ted Menten,
Gentle Closings

The desire to have a death of one's own is becoming more and more rare. In a short time it will be as rare as a life of one's own.

Rainer Maria Rilke

HELPING THE DYING AT HOME

Once, birth and death were home-centered everywhere, and they remain so in many countries still. But in some industrialized nations of the twentieth century, they were moved from the home to the hospital. Birth and death became medical procedures, managed by hospital personnel and protocol. . . .

But there's been a change. In recent years, parents and baby have come to take precedence over institutional policy and technological demands. Birth is again being seen as part of life, not a matter of medical procedure. . . . Many women are choosing to deliver at home, assisted by a birthing coach or midwife. When birth does take place in a hospital, it often occurs in birthing suites decorated to be cozier and more homelike than the usual sterile delivery room. . . .

Just so, the process of dying has begun to return to the "old-fashioned" way. Thanks to the rise of the hospice movement, the emphasis has shifted from professional providers of care and their tools to those most centrally involved—patient and informal caregiver, whether family or friend. As with childbirth, the care of the dying is now influenced as much as possible by those main players, who receive as much information as they want and need. Dying patients are seen less often as passive targets for diagnostic tests and painkillers, and more often as individuals with control over their living and dying.

Given the choice, most people prefer to die at home: most families prefer truthful reports on a terminal patient's condition. Though the idea of providing care at home for someone dying can be formidable and frightening, many families are able to handle it. With the proper training and support, they can learn the skills needed to keep a dying person comfortable—especially in light of advances in pain control that allow a layperson to administer medications that ease discomfort without drugging someone into a stupor. And, at the end, patients feel less isolated and fearful, while those present come away more comforted, knowing that they've participated as fully as possible in the death of someone they care about.

Though it can be grief- and stress-laden, death can occur in a context of completion and closure. After going through a death this way, many people say, "This may have been the hardest thing I've ever done, but I'm so glad I did it," or "The only thing that really helps me now that she's gone is that she knew as I do, that I did everything I could for her."

It's common, initially, for the family to greet the hospice nurse with a warning: "Don't say anything to her about dying. She doesn't know and she couldn't handle it!" Moments later, the patient tells the nurse privately: "Don't say anything to my family about my dying. They don't know and they couldn't handle it!" With support and encouragement both patient and family can end this compassionate conspiracy and move on to honest, open communication. . . . When dying people aren't allowed to talk about what's happening to them, they become lonely, even amid loving, concerned people. They may feel isolated and abandoned, and in turn become resentful and angry.

. . . Contrary to popular belief, or perhaps from wishful thinking—because of our own discomfort with death—dying people know they are dying, even if no one else knows or has told them.

. . . Dying people communicate in wondrous but sometimes strange ways, and it takes persistence and insight to catch and decipher their messages—which come by gesture, by facial expression, by allegory or symbol. Unfortunately, these messages are often missed or misinterpreted.

[The dying often use symbolic language—metaphors indicating preparation for a journey or change soon to happen—] to alert those around them that it is time for them to die. They also have a deep concern about the welfare of those they love, asking themselves, "Do they understand? Are they ready? Are they going to be all right?" It seems dying people need permission to die. If given, that permission provides great relief: its absence can make the dying process more difficult and lengthy. The dying intuitively know when—and often why—this permission is being withheld, by the behavior of those around them. This withholding indicates that those they love don't understand their struggle, nor are they prepared emotionally to deal with the finality of their leaving.

> Maggie Callanan and
> Patricia Kelley,
> *Final Gifts*

HELPING THE DYING

To learn really to help those who are dying is to begin to become fearless and responsible about our own dying, and to find in ourselves the beginnings of an unbounded compassion that we may never have suspected. . . .

The most essential thing in life is to establish an unafraid, heartfelt communication with others, and it is never more important than with a dying person. . . . Dying will bring out many repressed emotions: sadness or numbness or guilt, or even jealousy of those who are still well. Help the person not to repress these emotions when they rise. Be with the person as the waves of pain and grief break; with acceptance, time, and patient understanding, the emotions slowly subside and return the dying person to that ground of serenity, calm, and sanity that is most deeply and truly theirs.

Don't try to be too wise; don't always try to search for something profound to say. You don't have to *do* or say anything to make things better. Just be there as fully as you can. And if you are feeling a lot of anxiety and fear, and don't know what to do, admit that openly to the dying person and ask his or her help.

When the dying person is finally communicating his or her most private feelings, do not interrupt, deny, or diminish what the person is saying. The terminally ill or dying are in the most vulnerable situation of their lives, and you will need all your skill and resources of sensitivity, and warmth, and loving compassion to enable them to reveal themselves. Learn to listen, and learn to receive in silence: an open, calm silence that makes the other person feel accepted. Be as relaxed as you can, be at ease; sit there with your dying friend or relative as if you had nothing more important or enjoyable to do.

I have found that, as in all grave situations of life, two things are most useful: a common-sense approach and a sense of humor. Humor has a marvelous way of lightening the atmosphere, helping to put the process of dying in its true and universal perspective, and breaking the over-seriousness and intensity of the situation. Use humor, then, as skillfully and as gently as possible.

I have found also, from my own experience, that it is essential not to take anything too personally. When you least expect it, dying people can make you the target of all their anger and blame. As Elisabeth Kübler-Ross says, anger and blame can "be displaced in all directions, and projected onto the environment at times almost at random." Do not imagine that this rage is really aimed at you; realizing what fear and grief it springs from will stop you from reacting to it in ways that might damage your relationship.

Sometimes you may be tempted to preach to the dying, or to give them your own spiritual formula. Avoid this temptation absolutely, especially when you suspect that it is not what the dying person wants! No one wishes to be "rescued" with someone else's beliefs. Remember your task is not to convert anyone to anything, but to help the person in front of you get in touch with his or her own strength, confidence, faith, and spirituality, whatever that might be. Of course, if the person is really open to spiritual matters, and really wants to know what you think about them, don't hold back either. . . .

Being aware of your own fears about dying will help you immeasurably to be aware of the fears of the dying person. Just imagine deeply what those might be: fear of increasing, uncontrolled pain, fear of suffering, fear of indignity, fear of dependence, fear that the lives we have led have been meaningless, fear of separation from all we love, fear of losing control, fear of losing respect; perhaps our greatest fear of all is fear of fear itself, which grows more and more powerful the more we evade it.

Usually when you feel fear, you feel isolated and alone, and without company. But when somebody keeps company with you and talks of his or her own fears, then you realize fear is universal and the edge, the personal pain, is taken off it. Your fears are brought back to the human and universal context. Then you are able to understand, be more compassionate, and deal with your own fears in a much more positive and inspiring way.

As you grow to confront and accept your own fears, you will become increasingly sensitive to those of the person before you, and you will find you develop the intelligence and insight to help that person to bring his or her fears out into the open, deal with them, and begin skillfully to dispel them. For facing your fears, you will find, will not only make you more compassionate and braver and clearer; it will also make you more skillful, and that skillfulness will open to you all kinds of ways of enabling the dying to understand and face themselves.

It is not only the tensions that you have to learn to let go of, but the dying person as well. If you are attached and cling to the dying person, you can bring him or her a lot of unnecessary heartache and make it very hard for the person to let go and die peacefully. . . . Some families resist letting their loved one go, thinking that to do so is a betrayal, and a sign that they don't love them enough. Christine Longaker tells these families to imagine that they are in the place of the one who is dying. "Imagine you are standing on the deck of an ocean liner, about to set sail. You look back on the shore and see all your family and friends waving goodbye. You have no choice about leaving, and the ship is already moving away. How would you want the people you loved to be saying goodbye to you? What would help you most on your journey?"

There is no greater gift of charity you can give than helping a person to die well.

Sogyal Rinpoche,
*The Tibetan Book of Living
and Dying*

We need, in love, to practice only this:
letting each other go. For holding on
comes easily; we do not need to learn it.

Rainer Maria Rilke,
from "Requiem"

I Have Never Felt
More Alive

I have never felt more alive than during the months Jim was dying. Home was a precipice, a place where the air was thin, but the view revealed truths I had never before known. At times, I felt drenched with insight.

There was a fullness to the days, a sharpness of focus. In that climate, I discovered my bare self. Where some might have seen only bruises, I felt a ripening.

Even when most afraid, I could wrap my arm around Jim and find relief in the simple act of touching his face or rubbing his hand. When I sighed, he was there, taking my broken pieces and cradling them in his heart. Our lives were propelled not by promise, but by rich moments that offered everything from giddiness to grace.

❧

The cancer had come suddenly, insinuating itself into our lives like an unexpected house guest. It arrived unbidden, a stranger. But before long it was to clutch us in its embrace like the closest of intimates. Slowly and silently it stole Jim's life, and forever changed mine. . . . We became ardent students of cancer, believing that if we got to know it well enough we could somehow outsmart it. . . . Radiation treatments took place in a doctor's office, where we'd see the same patients every day, mostly old people or women with breast cancer. Somehow, their tragedies seemed worse than ours. In the waiting room, under a poster that advised "Eat! Eat! Eat!" folks talked amicably about food tolerance, vitamins, pain medication and, sometimes, the sorry specifics of their disease. I tried to shut out their voices, burying my face in a magazine in the farthest corner of the room. I felt safer that way. It wasn't the kind of place where I wanted to stand out. I didn't want to be one of them. . . .

ᘏᙓ

As we went into February, it seemed we had never known anything but the cancer, so connected were we to it. Time developed a sharpness. Moments somehow seemed larger. We were weighted in the present in a landscape that, while unfamiliar and disquieting, had a depth that was extraordinarily vivid and illuminative. As we searched our hearts for understanding, we discovered a simple sweetness to life, a holiness almost. I have never felt closer to a human being than I did to Jim during those months. . . .

ᘏᙓ

[They move to San Francisco, stopping in Carmel on the way.]

As I drove the narrow, winding Pacific Coast Highway toward Carmel, Jim sat hunched over in the back seat, his eyes clamped shut, his face plowed with pain. I tried to ignore him, preferring the serenity of the shoreline to the sight of the sick man in my rear-view mirror.

"Open your eyes and enjoy the goddamn ride," I

screamed finally, adding a silent postscript: "You'll never see this again."

I wanted to tell Jim that I was scared, that fear had burrowed so deep in my gut I couldn't even find it. I wanted to ask, "Are you afraid of dying? What does it feel like?" I wanted to say, "How dare you leave me now!" I wanted to know: Would he miss me? But all I could do was yell and all he could do was weep.

The cancer was like a second skin, a shadow we couldn't shake. In a way, I was jealous because there were times when Jim seemed closer to it than to me. We had always been able to talk to each other but, with the cancer wedged between us, I choked on the words I most wanted to say. I was afraid that if I started to talk I wouldn't be able to stop. I drove into a scenic overlook and crawled into the back seat with Jim. He popped a couple of pain pills and I took his hand. His body was trembling. I have never felt more ashamed.

✺

. . . I hounded Jim like a drill sergeant to eat, but my presence at the bedroom door with yet another chocolate fudge pudding cup was clearly unwelcome. . . . Food became a real issue, a power struggle that bloodied us both. Jim was frustrated he couldn't eat and I took his refusal to do so as a personal rebuke. We each felt we had failed the other. I wish now I had let up on him.

✺

During April, the hospital became the center of everything we knew and hoped for. A part of me felt like I was

betraying Jim every time I walked outside into the sunshine. The world had started to look different: Colors
were richer, the landscape fuller, the air fresher. A part
of me yearned to get out, to walk unencumbered, to
soak in a world that wasn't governed by nursing shifts,
medication schedules and doctors' rounds.

We watched TV, read the papers and got to know the
guts of the eleventh floor: We learned which nurses gave
the best needle sticks; which patients were waiting for
bone marrow transplants (there were three); and which
doctors were courageous enough to be compassionate. I
liked the hospital.

⁓

[Finally, Jim comes home to die.]

I began to miss Jim even before he died. One of the
most difficult things I've ever done was to sing "Happy
Birthday" to him on his 41st birthday, knowing it would
be his last. . . . In those final days, he fixated on the
yellow alarm clock and the TV remote controller—I
think because they represented order and control, elements that had disappeared from his own life.

⁓

On the spring afternoon that he died, I was sitting at the
dining-room table when I heard Jim's parents call me to
his bedside.

I didn't know Jim was dead until Agnes walked over
and closed his eyes. An older woman, calm and efficient,
Agnes took care of Jim during the four days before he
died.

"This is it?" I thought to myself. "That's Jim and he's dead? That's his body and it's dead?"

I keep remembering Jim's eyes—like a deer's caught in a headlight. In those moments before he died, he seemed focused on a singular object no one else could see. I hope he wasn't frightened.

✳

I always think of the day Jim died as the great divide in my life, harshly measuring everything into The Before and The After.

Ellen Uzelac,
*Lost & Found: A Journey
Through Grief*

The closest bonds we will ever know are bonds of grief. The deepest community one of sorrow.

Cormac McCarthy,
All the Pretty Horses

I'd been there a few minutes, setting up command, when Roger began to moan. It was the saddest, hollowest sound I've ever heard, and loud, like the trumpet note of a wounded animal. It had no shape to it, nothing like a word, and he repeated it over and over, every few seconds. "Why is he doing that?" I asked the nurse, but she didn't know. I assumed he must be roaring with misery and anxiety, and he hadn't had any Xanax since the previous day. I ordered a tranquilizer and told him everything I was doing. It wasn't till ten weeks later, on New Year's Day, that I understood the trumpet sound. I was crying up at the grave, and started to mimic his moaning, and suddenly understood that what he was doing was calling my name. Nothing in my life or the death to come hurts as much as that, him calling me without a voice through a wall he could not pierce.

Within fifteen minutes the intern came in with a shot to relax him, and right after that they began the ampho drip. I was on the phone to Jaimee constantly, the two of us gnawing our hearts as we waited to see if he'd have convulsions. Meanwhile the nurse taught me to communicate with Rog by telling him to blink when I asked him a question. *Can you hear me, Rog?* And his eyelids fluttered. It was such a stunning gift to have him back, tapping through the wall like that. Thirty or forty times in the next hour I made him do it again, lobbing him yes questions and cheering at the reassuring flutter of his eyelids. I kept telling him how much of the drug still had to go in. I talked and talked, excitedly declaring that we were home free. It was working. We were going to bring him back. I held the phone so Jaimee could talk in his ear, and he blinked to say he heard her.

I don't regret a syllable of our manic cheer. I wouldn't have wanted the last he heard from me to be moaning and grief. We were pulling through, as we always did. I asked a friend with a thousand nights' experience of young men dying, How much pain was Roger in that last twenty-four hours? I've heard all the tales of the tribe now about the pounding headaches of crypto. He said the harder thing for Roger than the pain would surely have been the consciousness of his final imprisonment and exile from me. I know he's right because it comes to me in nightmares over and over, the last claustrophobia, no way to touch your friend again or say good-bye as you spiral down. At least we had that queer and eloquent hour of the eyelids, and then he fell asleep.

> Paul Monette,
> *Borrowed Time: An AIDS Memoir*

We are stretched to meet a new dimension
Of love, a more demanding range
Where despair and hope must intertwine.
How grow to meet it? Intention
Here can neither move nor change
The raw truth. Death is on the line.
It comes to separate and estrange
Lover from lover in some reckless design.
Where do we go from here?

Fear. Fear. Fear. Fear.

Our world has never been more stark
Or more in peril.
It is very lonely now in the dark.
Lonely and sterile.

And yet in the simple turn of a head
Mercy lives. I heard it when someone said
"I must go now to a dying friend.
Every night at nine I tuck him into bed,

And give him a shot of morphine.''
And added, ''I go where I have never been.''
I saw he meant into a new discipline
He had not imagined before, and a new grace.

Every day now we meet it face to face.
Every day now devotion is the test.
Through the long hours, the hard, caring nights
We are forging a new union. We are blest.

As closed hands open to each other
Closed lives open to strange tenderness.
We are learning the hard way how to mother.
Who says it is easy? But we have the power.
I watch the faces deepen all around me.
It is the time of change, the saving hour.
The word is not fear, the word we live,
But an old word suddenly made new,
As we learn it again, as we bring it alive:

Love. Love. Love. Love.

> May Sarton,
> ''AIDS''

Be careful, then, and be gentle about death.
For it is hard to die, it is difficult to go through
the door, even when it opens.

And the poor dead, when they have left the walled
and silvery city of the now hopeless body
where are they to go, Oh where are they to go?

They linger in the shadow of the earth.
The earth's long conical shadow is full of souls
that cannot find a way across the sea of change.

Be kind, Oh be kind to your dead
and give them a little encouragement
and help them to build their little ship of death.

For the soul has a long, long journey after death
to the sweet home of pure oblivion.
Each needs a little ship, a little ship
and the proper store of meal for the longest journey.

Oh, from out of your heart
provide for your dead once more, equip them
like departing mariners, lovingly.

> D. H. Lawrence,
> "All Souls' Day"

THE EXPERIENCE OF DYING

Different Responses to Dying

. . . Each individual tends to die as he or she has lived, especially as he or she has previously reacted in periods of threat, stress, failure, challenge, shock and loss. . . . Roughly speaking, the course of an individual's life while he or she is dying over time, say of cancer, duplicates or mirrors or parallels the course of the life during its ''dark periods''; that is, one dies as one has lived in the terrible moments of one's life.

Edwin Shneidman,
Voices of Death

I believe that death is a friend, a fabulous dancer who will twirl me away in my last waltz.

Ted Menten,
Gentle Closings

One cannot be honest even at the end of one's life, for no one is wholly alone. We are bound to those we love, or to those who love us, and to those who need us to be brave, or content, or even happy enough to allow them not to worry about us. So we must refrain from giving pain, as our last gift to our fellows.

Florida Scott-Maxwell,
The Measure of My Days

That is what they call being reconciled to die. They call it reconciled when pain has strummed a symphony of suffering back and forth across you, up and down, round and round you until each little fiber is worn tissue-thin with aching. And when you are lying beaten, and buffeted, battered and broken—pain goes out, joins hands with Death and comes back to dance, dance, dance, stamp, stamp, stamp down on you until you give up.

Marita Bonner,
Frye Street and Environs

She had supposed that on her deathbed, she would have something final to tell her children when they gathered round. But nothing was final. She didn't have anything to tell them. She felt a kind of shyness; she felt inadequate.

Anne Tyler,
Dinner at the Homesick Restaurant

She wore
her coming death
as gracefully
as if it were a coat
she'd learned to sew.
When it grew cold enough
she'd simply button it
and go.

> Linda Pastan,
> "Caroline"

For my part, I would like to die fully conscious that I am dying . . . slow enough to allow death to insinuate itself into my body and fully unfold, so as not to miss the ultimate experience, the passage.

> Marguerite Yourcenar,
> *With Open Eyes*

AFRAID—BUT OF WHAT?

I don't think people are afraid of death. What they are afraid of is the incompleteness of their life.

> A 30-year-old man dying of
> leukemia, in *Death and the*
> *Creative Life* by Lisl Goodman

. . . It is hard for most of us to contemplate our death without being scared of it. We are scared of annihilation and of non-being. We are scared of going into the unknown. We are scared of an afterlife where we may have to pay for our sins. We are scared of being helplessly alone. There are many, it is said, who fear the agonies of a last illness, whose fear is of dying—not of being dead. But it also has been said that we carry within us, all of our life, a dread of abandonment.

Our earliest separations, it is argued, have given us all our first, bitter foretaste of death. And our later encounters with death—with death down the road or with death knocking at our door—revive the terrors of those first separations.

Judith Viorst,
Necessary Losses

What, then, does it mean to die? I need a new word, somewhere between the words "fear" and "dread." Perhaps the word "anguish" comes closest. What anguishes me the most is the idea of naughtment: to abandon my loved ones, to disappear as though I had never been . . .

Edwin Shneidman,
Voices of Death

I fear pain, dependency, ugliness, and loss of control. Pity from others. Being tolerated. Doctors with tubes and shots and knives and drugs. I want my dignity! I don't want to crap my bed as my last act and be remembered wasted and helpless. I don't trust others to let me die in good season; I'm afraid they'll keep me alive as a semblance out of misguided love or duty. *Spare me duty.* . . . I'm terrified to *die*—something in me is *terrified* of how I'll behave during the process. Will I wipe out all good memories in the minds of those who know me to the end? Will I snivel? Or scream? Will I be a toothless hag? Who will wipe my ass? . . . I don't trust my strength not to be disgusting. . . . On another level, I want to avoid death at all costs. . . . I need more time. I need more time. . . .

> Peg Elliott Mayo,
> in *Mortal Acts* by
> David Feinstein
> and Peg Elliott Mayo

Some fear that death will come too soon, before they are ready. Some fear that it will not come soon enough, that they will be too old to face it independently.

I Had One Fear

My only fear about death is that it will not come soon enough. Life still interests and occupies me. Happily I am not in such discomfort that I wish for death, I love and am loved, but please God I die before I lose my independence. I do not know what I believe about life after death; if it exists then I burn with interest, if not—well,

I am tired. I have endured the flame of living and that should be enough. . . .

I had one fear. What if something went wrong, and I became an invalid? What if I became a burden, ceased to be a person and became a problem, a patient, someone who could not die? That was my one fear, but my chances were reasonably good, so all was simple and settled and out of my hands. Being ill in a nursing home became my next task, a sombre dance in which I knew some of the steps. I must conform. I must be correct. I must be meek, obedient and grateful, on no account must I be surprising. If I deviated by the breadth of a toothbrush I would be in the wrong. . . .

I don't like to write this down, yet it is much in the minds of the old. We wonder how much older we have to become, and what degree of decay we may have to endure. We keep whispering to ourselves, "Is this age yet? How far must I go?" For age can be dreaded more than death. "How many years of vacuity? To what degree of deterioration must I advance?" Some want death now, as release from old age, some say they will accept death willingly, but in a few years. I feel the solemnity of death, and the possibility of some form of continuity. Death feels a friend because it will release us from the deterioration of which we cannot see the end. It is waiting for death that wears us down, and the distaste for what we may become. . . .

But we also find that as we age we are more alive than seems likely, convenient, or even bearable. Too often our problem is the fervour of life within us. My dear fellow octogenarians, how are we to carry so much life, and what are we to do with it? . . . When truly old, too frail to use the vigour that pulses in us, and weary, sometimes even scornful of what can seem the pointless activity of mankind, we may sink down to some deeper level and find a new supply of life that amazes us.

. . . *It has taken me* all the time I've had to become myself, yet now that I am old there are times when I feel I am barely here, no room for me at all. I remember that in the last months of my pregnancies the child seemed to claim almost all my body, my strength, my breath, and I held on wondering if my burden was my enemy, uncertain as to whether my life was at all mine. Is life a pregnancy? That would make death a birth.

Florida Scott-Maxwell,
The Measure of My Days

COUNTERING THE FEAR OF DEATH

Life is a great surprise: I do not see why death should not be an even greater one.
Vladimir Nabokov

Death belongs to life as birth does.
The walk is in the raising of the foot as in the laying of it down.
Rabindranath Tagore,
Stray Birds

To fear death, gentlemen, is nothing other than to think oneself wise when one is not; for it is to think one knows what one does not know. No man knows whether death may not even turn out to be the greatest of blessings for a human being; and yet people fear it as if they knew for certain that it is the greatest of evils.

Socrates,
Plato's *Apology*

Perhaps the best cure for the fear of death is to reflect that life has a beginning as well as an end. There was a time when we were not: this gives us no concern—why then should it trouble us that a time will come when we shall cease to be?

William Hazlitt

Death does not have to be a catastrophic, destructive thing: indeed it can be viewed as one of the most constructive, positive, and creative elements of culture and life.

Elisabeth Kübler-Ross

All goes onward and outward,
Nothing collapses
And to die is different from
What anyone supposes
And luckier.

Walt Whitman

DYING MAY NOT BE
SO BAD, AFTER ALL

We have as much distaste for talking about personal death as for thinking about it; it is an indelicacy, like talking in mixed company about venereal disease or abortion in the old days. Death on a grand scale does not bother us in the same special way: we can sit around a dinner table and discuss war, involving 60 million volatilized human deaths, as though we were talking about bad weather; we can watch abrupt bloody death every day, in color, on films and television, without blinking back a tear. It is when the numbers of dead are very small, and very close, that we begin to think in scurrying circles. At the very center of the problem is the naked cold deadness of one's own self, the only reality in nature of which we can have absolute certainty, and it is unmentionable, unthinkable. We may be even less willing to face the issue at first hand than our predecessors because of a secret new hope that maybe it will go away. . . .

There are signs that medicine may be taking a new interest in the process, partly from curiosity, partly from an embarrassed realization that we have not been handling this aspect of disease with as much skill as physicians once displayed, back in the days before they became convinced that disease was their solitary and sometimes defeatable enemy. It used to be the hardest and most important of all the services of a good doctor to be on hand at the time of death and to provide comfort, usually in the home. Now it is done in hospitals, in secrecy (one of the reasons for the increased fear of death these days may be that so many people are totally unfamiliar with it; they never actually see it happen in real life). Some of our technology permits us to deny its existence, and we maintain flickers of life for long stretches in one community of cells or another, as though we were keeping a flag flying. Death is not a sudden-all-at-once affair; cells go down in sequence, one by one. You can, if you like, recover great numbers of them many hours after the lights have gone out, and grow them out in cultures. It takes hours, even days, before the irreversible word finally gets around to all the provinces.

We may be about to rediscover that dying is not such a bad thing to do after all. Sir William Osler took this view: he disapproved of people who spoke of the agony of death, maintaining that there was no such thing.

In a nineteenth-century memoir on an expedition in Africa, there is a story by David Livingston about his own experience of near-death. He was caught by a lion, crushed across the chest in the animal's great jaws, and saved in the instant by a lucky shot from a friend. Later, he remembered the episode in clear detail. He was so amazed by the extraordinary sense of peace, calm, and total painlessness associated with being killed that he constructed a theory that all creatures are provided with a protective physiologic mechanism, switched on at the verge of death, carrying them through in a haze of tranquillity.

I have seen agony in death only once, in a patient with

rabies; he remained acutely aware of every stage in the process of his own disintegration over a twenty-four-hour period, right up to his final moment. It was as though, in the special neuropathology of rabies, the switch had been prevented from turning.

We will be having new opportunities to learn more about the physiology of death at first hand, from the increasing numbers of cardiac patients who have been through the whole process and then back again. . . . Those who remember parts or all of their episodes do not recall any fear, or anguish. Several people who remained conscious throughout, while appearing to have been quite dead, could only describe a remarkable sensation of detachment. One man underwent coronary occlusion with cessation of the heart and dropped for all practical purposes dead, in front of a hospital; within a few minutes his heart had been restarted by electrodes and he breathed his way back into life. According to his account, the strangest thing was that there were so many people around him, moving so urgently, handling his body with such excitement, while all his awareness was of quietude. . . .

I find myself surprised by the thought that dying is an all-right thing to do, but perhaps it should not surprise. It is, after all, the most ancient and fundamental of biologic functions, with its mechanisms worked out with the same attention to detail, the same provision for the advantage of the organism, the same abundance of genetic information for guidance through the stages, that we have long since become accustomed to finding in all the crucial acts of living.

Lewis Thomas,
The Lives of a Cell

TRY TO UNDERSTAND ME

Often we forget that the dying are losing their whole world: their house, their job, their relationships, their body, and their mind—they're losing everything. All the losses we could possibly experience in life are joined together in one overwhelming loss when we die, so how could anyone dying not be sometimes sad, sometimes panicked, sometimes angry? Elisabeth Kübler-Ross suggests five stages in the process of coming to terms with dying: denial, anger, bargaining, depression, and acceptance. Of course not everyone will go through all these stages, or necessarily in this order: and for some people the road to acceptance may be an extremely long and thorny one; others may not reach acceptance at all. Ours is a culture that does not give people very much true perspective on their thoughts, emotions, and experiences, and many people facing death and its final challenge find themselves feeling cheated by their own ignorance, and terribly frustrated and angry, especially since no one seems to want to comprehend them and their most heartfelt needs. As Cicely Saunders, the great pioneer of the hospice movement in Britain, writes: "I once asked a man who knew he was dying what he needed above all in those who were caring for him. He said, 'For someone to look as if they are trying to understand me.' Indeed, it is impossible to understand fully another person, but I never forgot that he did not ask for success but only that someone should care enough to try."

Sogyal Rinpoche,
The Tibetan Book of Living and Dying

A RELUCTANT DEATH

He talks himself up like this all evening. He extols the virtues of the new portable telephone he bought for 129 pounds just before going into hospital—"you can take it two hundred yards down the garden—it'll be useful when I'm lying out in summer, or next back-end when I'm raking leaves." He tells me about the new headlamps he's ordered for when he's fit to drive again, for when he goes back to hospital to have his stitches out in a couple of weeks. There is tenacity in all this denial, some deep will to survive, and we collude in it. My mother teases him—"We've not had him climbing any hills yet, but tomorrow maybe"—and runs her fingers through his hair. I imagine him reaching Christmas at any rate, two and a half weeks away—wrapped in his red tartan blanket smiling bravely while the children open their presents, sad to think there may be no more Christmases but appeased by the joy and continuity around him. I had come up half-ready to spend longer than the weekend here, but there's no immediate panic. At ten he goes to bed, tottering off like a toddler in its mother's high-heeled shoes. I ring my wife and tell her to expect me the following evening. . . .

Sunday morning, and I can hear my father's voice as I wake. He has just had my mother make him a second breakfast: the spoonful of Complan wasn't enough, he wanted a quarter cup of cornflakes too. Now he feels in need of a shower, and I fit a new light-bulb in the cubicle for him as he soft-shouts the instructions from the bed: "Twist the old light-bulb in and leftwards to release it. Got it? Right, now push the new one in and rightwards to insert it." Is it that he assumes I still don't know how to change a light-bulb? Or that his is the one infallible method, the beautiful simplicity of which he thinks the rest of the world hasn't yet cottoned on to? I take heart from my irritation: he must be feeling better. . . .

For the last few days, my father, whenever he sits on the edge of the bed and Nikki comes running, has had to spread his hands out in front of him (as if warming them on the fire) to stop the dog jumping into his naked lap, and the dog has slunk away, not used to such rejection. But his animal bewilderment isn't so different from our own informed incomprehension. . . .

"At least it wasn't like blowing up the tram in Bolton," says my sister, coaxingly, prompting him to embark on another old story, about how he and two schoolfriends raided the chemistry lab and laid some explosive they'd mixed on the tramlines in Bolton. We know the tale by heart—the loud bang, the tram-driver scratching his head, the traffic brought to a standstill, the pranksters sneaking away unnoticed. To hear him tell it is comforting—for a moment, death seems to have receded. But then again, not: for us to cajole him into telling stories which we've spent most of our lives being bored or exasperated by is a sign of how desperate we've become, how little we believe we'll ever hear them—or him—again. It's like the ornaments or pictures on the wall I've always hated, the lolling dogs, cutesy goose-girls and naff souvenirs, suddenly precious now. We don't want different stories; we want the same stories. And it doesn't matter what he says, only that he says something: now that everything is a last thing, even the most banal utterance is depth-charged. . . .

On her long dressing-table stool at the end of the bed, my mother and I discuss funeral arrangements. We're nervous with each other, not sure if this is the right way to go about things, prefacing each new item—the wake, the will, what to do with his ashes—with ''I'm sorry, it sounds macabre, but . . .'' His dying is all we can think about, but is talking about it immoral, inauspicious, defeatist? She tells me how at his insistence she phoned the garage this morning to see if the new headlamps had come in and how they've just rung back and quoted seventy pounds—at which point my father wakes and says, ''I'm sure Halfords could do it cheaper,'' then goes off again. We snigger at how the word *garage* sparked him into consciousness, whereas he'd slept through *coffin* and *crematorium*. Or is he just pretending not to hear? Mothers shut out the memory of childbirth pain once labour is over: my father has blanked off the diagnosis of ten days ago in much the same way. He can't hear the word *death* because he knows he's getting better. . . .

There are to be no more moments of lucidity, no more conversations, only the look of him all afternoon and evening: the stubble, the left eye half-open, the head sunk on his chest until some word in whatever anecdote we are trying to engage him with—my train journey up, my mother's dealings with the gardener—seems to catch and snag for a second, to trip some not always related words of his own, then to ratchet away hopelessly into space again. Yesterday he had drunk some milk and asked: "Can I have some more wine?" Even that sort of irreality, that hallucidity, seems unattainable now. . . .

Then we slide the new nappy [diaper] under him, my sister proficient at one side, my mother—a fifties terry-nappy mother—struggling with the technology at the other. I have to slide my right arm through my father's right arm and across his chest to support him under the left arm, while with my free left arm I hold the nappy firm so my mother can stick down the tie. Now he is done, and I begin to lift and turn him in a semicircle back again. But to do this means moving the chair with my knee, and I miscue and tilt it, and for one horrible moment one of its legs catches his leg, spearing the instep, pressing hard into the puffiness, skewering him to the floor, enough for him to mumble: "Chair." Then I see and lift it off again, and I get him up and then recumbent on the bed, his chest vertical, the pillows propped behind him. And I sit there breathing heavily, his hand in my hand, wondering if he, being the patriarch he was, ever changed a nappy of mine, and wondering if this might be a definition of what it is to be grown up—not changing your child's nappy but changing your parent's.

> Blake Morrison,
> *And When Did You Last See*
> *Your Father?*

It's not that I'm afraid to die, I just don't want to be there when it happens.

> Woody Allen,
> *Getting Even*

DENIAL

People who are dying use denial to protect themselves from information too painful to absorb. Eventually most of them will move from denial to acceptance, although they will often go back and forth. And some people will hang on to denial right to the end. They don't need other people to force them to face reality.

Tonight, when Mom went to bed, I noticed that she put her dentures on the night table. I remembered how this time last year she balked at removing them even for surgery, saying that no one, including Dad, had ever seen her without teeth and she wanted to keep it that way. But now she has lost so much weight that the dentures don't fit well. The loose fit irritates her gums and makes eating difficult, but she is not strong enough to undergo the process of getting fitted for new ones. . . . This spring Mom was willing to endure extreme pain in order to go to the beauty parlor "for Dad." She has fought hard to maintain her vanity throughout this ordeal, and now it is being wrenched from her. That, more than any other loss, puts her and Dad in different worlds. Dad is among the living. Mom belongs to the dying. I think they have each accepted that in the last two weeks.

Mom doesn't talk about dying though. She talks about getting better and is dismayed that it is taking so long. Mike thinks that if her stoicism and denial have lasted this long, through such extremity, they will last to the final moment. She will believe that she is going to be fine, that bad things don't really happen to good people, that she is not going to die, right up until the second of her death. I don't believe that. But neither do I understand how she can maintain hope as she does in the face of such assaults upon her well-being.

> Le Anne Schreiber,
> *Midstream*

The problem, for people who are dying, is when they sense that those around them—and sometimes it is the doctor—will feel more comfortable if they maintain the pretense that they are going to get better, that they haven't stopped fighting or "given up hope." Sherwin Nuland, in How We Die, *relates his own painful experience playing the denial game.*

Although there was no doubt that [my Aunt] Rose knew she was dying of cancer, we never spoke of it to her, nor did she bring it up. She worried about us and we worried about her, each side certain it would be too much for the other to bear. We knew the outlook and so did she; we convinced ourselves she didn't know, though we sensed that she did, as she must have convinced herself we didn't know, though she must have known we did. So it was like the old scenario that so often throws a shadow over the last days of people with cancer: we knew—she knew—we knew she knew—she knew we knew—and none of us would talk about it when we were all together. We kept up the charade to the end. Aunt Rose was deprived and so were we of the coming together that should have been, when we might finally tell her what her life had given us. In this sense, my Aunt Rose died alone.

Without perhaps even realizing it, we had committed one of the worst of the errors that can be made during terminal illness—all of us, Rose included, had decided incorrectly and in opposition to every principle of our lives together that it was more important to protect one another from the open admission of a painful truth than it was to achieve a final sharing that might have snatched an enduring comfort and even some dignity from the anguishing fact of death. We denied ourselves what should have been ours.

Sherwin Nuland,
How We Die

HOPE

Hope tends to persist through all the stages of dying, although it comes and goes. Sometimes the sheer will to live carries people through against impossible odds. Surely the few who survived the Nazi death camps never gave up hope.

The sun has made a veil of gold
So lovely that my body aches
Above, the heavens shriek with blue
Convinced I've smiled by some mistake.
The world's abloom and seems to smile.
I want to fly but where, how high?
If in barbed wire, things can bloom
Why couldn't I? I will not die!

Anonymous, 1944
"On a Sunny Evening"

Hope is the thing with feathers
That perches in the soul,
And sings the tune without the words,
And never stops at all.

Emily Dickinson

Faith
is the bird
that feels the light
And sings

when the dawn
is still dark.

Rabindranath Tagore

Hope is hearing the melody of the future; faith is dancing
to it today.

Ruben A. Alvez,
quoted by Molly Fumia in
*Safe Passage: Words to Help the
Grieving Hold Fast and Let Go*

ANGER

*In people who are terminally ill, write Maggie Callanan and
Patricia Kelley in* Final Gifts, *the roots of anger "often are
frustration, resentment, or fear. Frustration can stem from help-
lessness at losing control and becoming dependent on others;
resentment, from seeing others' lives go on; fear, from uncer-
tainty about what dying is like." Dylan Thomas, during his
father's final illness, saw anger as an appropriate response, one
he wished for his father.*

Do not go gentle into that good night,
Old age should burn and rave at close of day;
Rage, rage against the dying of the light.

Though wise men at their end know dark is right,
Because their words had forked no lightning they
Do not go gentle into that good night.

Good men, the last wave by, crying how bright
Their frail deeds might have danced in a green bay,
Rage, rage against the dying of the light.

Wild men who caught and sang the sun in flight,
And learn, too late, they grieved it on its way,
Do not go gentle into that good night.

Grave men, near death, who see with blinding sight
Blind eyes could blaze like meteors and be gay,
Rage, rage against the dying of the light.

And you, my father, there on the sad height,
Curse, bless, me now with your fierce tears, I pray.
Do not go gentle into that good night.
Rage, rage against the dying of the light.

> Dylan Thomas,
> "Do Not Go Gentle into That
> Good Night"

Leonard Matlovich, an Air Force Tech Sergeant who did three tours in Vietnam, later died of AIDS. Anger gives power to the epitaph on his gravestone in Congressional Cemetery, in Washington, D.C.

When I was in the military
They gave me a medal for killing two men
And a discharge for loving one.

> A Gay Vietnam Veteran

ACCEPTANCE

Acceptance is a quiet feeling of peaceful resignation, which may come and go but comes especially when death is close. With acceptance comes withdrawal and detachment, which can feel painful to those close to the dying person.

At the beginning of [*Stay of Execution,*] I described the trapped and desperate feeling that came over me after I had been told that I would die quite soon. Last Saturday night, when I felt so sick, I felt rather sure that I would die quite soon, and perhaps very soon, within the next day or so. I did not at all welcome the prospect, but it filled me with no sense of panic. I kissed Tish a fond good night at ten, took some Benadryl, and went easily off to sleep. Why the difference? . . .

Since mid-March, when the fevers and the night sweats began, I have written my column for *Newsweek* and worked on this book and driven downtown to dictate letters to Amanda, make telephone calls, and make dates for business lunches. Tish and I, as usual better guests than hosts, have gone out to dinner several times a week and talked and laughed with friends. I have lived, in short, what John Glick calls ''a normal life.''

But it has not been altogether normal. It is not normal to wake up every night just before dawn, with a fever of 101 or so, take a couple of pills, and settle down to sweat like a hog for four or five hours. It is not normal to feel so weak you can't play tennis or go trout fishing. And it is not normal either to feel a sort of creeping weariness and a sense of being terribly dependent, like a vampire, on the blood of others. After eight weeks of this kind of "normal" life, the thought of death loses some of its terror.

But the most important reason why I felt no panic fear last Saturday was, I think, the strange, unconscious, indescribable process which I have tried to describe in this book—the process of adjustment whereby one comes to terms with death. A dying man needs to die, as a sleepy man needs to sleep, and there comes a time when it is wrong, as well as useless, to resist.

Stewart Alsop,
Stay of Execution

Come lovely and soothing death,
Undulate round the world, serenely arriving, arriving,
In the day, in the night, to all, to each,
Sooner or later, delicate death.

Walt Whitman

Death is as necessary to the constitution as sleep; we shall rise refreshed in the morning.

Benjamin Franklin

Death is a natural part of life, which we will all surely have to face sooner or later. To my mind, there are two ways we can deal with it while we are alive. We can either choose to ignore it or we can confront the prospect of our own death and, by thinking clearly about it, try to minimise the suffering that it can bring. However, in neither of these ways can we actually overcome it.

As a Buddhist, I view death as a normal process, a reality that I accept will occur as long as I remain in this earthly existence. Knowing that I cannot escape it, I see no point in worrying about it. I tend to think of death as being like changing your clothes when they are old and worn out, rather than as some final end. Yet death is unpredictable: We do not know when or how it will take place. So it is only sensible to take certain precautions before it actually happens.

Naturally, most of us would like to die a peaceful death, but it is also clear that we cannot hope to die peacefully if our lives have been full of violence, or if our minds have mostly been agitated by emotions like anger, attachment, or fear. So if we wish to die well, we must learn how to live well: Hoping for a peaceful death, we must cultivate peace in our mind, and in our way of life.

From the Buddhist point of view, the actual experience of death is very important. Although how or where we will be reborn is generally dependent on karmic forces, our state of mind at the time of death can influence the quality of our next rebirth. So at the moment of death, in spite of the great variety of karmas we have accumulated, if we make a special effort to generate a virtuous state of mind, we may strengthen and activate a virtuous karma, and so bring about a happy rebirth.

The Dalai Lama,
in the foreword to
The Tibetan Book of Living and Dying

LETTING GO OF CONTROL

The Chinese poet and sage Chuang-tzu speaks of a man crossing a river in his boat. As he is navigating through the waters he notices another boat coming his way. As he thinks he sees someone in the oncoming boat he yells, "Steer aside!" and gesticulates and swears as the boat continues toward him.

But Chuang-tzu suggests we imagine that same fellow crossing the stream when he looks up to yell at the person in the other boat and discovers the boat is empty. "Even though he be a bad-tempered man he will not become very angry." The boat is being carried toward him by the currents, but since there is no one in the boat he is not threatened or angered. It's just an empty boat. And as the boat approaches he skillfully puts his oar out to steer the other boat aside so that a collision will not damage either vessel.

Chuang-tzu suggests that we empty our boat. That we relate to the world from that openhearted emptiness that flows with what is, so that nothing that comes out of us will be coming from the "someone-ness" which opposes the flow. That we let go of control of the world and come fully into being.

As soon as the mind's conditioning to be someone arises, a kind of pain comes into our heart. A feeling of being alone. It is the loneliness of our separateness. Our alienation from the universal. But when we sit quietly with that loneliness and let it float in the mind it dissolves into an "aloneness" which is not lonely. But is rather a recognition that we are each alone in the One. It is the great silence of the universe "alone" in space. It has a wholeness about it. But to change the intense loneliness of our personal isolation into an "aloneness with God," we must gently let go of control and stop re-creating the imagined self. We must surrender our specialness, our competition, our comparing minds.

Control is our attempt to make the world align with our personal desires. To let go of control is to go beyond the personal and merge with the universal.

Control creates bondage. Control is the defender of the clinging mind. It opposes the openness of the heart. If our boats are empty, though there is still a vessel carried by the prevailing winds and currents there is not "someone" in it to be misunderstood. There is no one to oppose. There is simply empty space, boat, water, wind. Everything is in perfect harmony. Nothing is pulling against the natural flow. No one in the boat: no one to suffer.

Chuang-tzu wrote of the ease that comes about when we let go of control and tune to what the ancient Chinese called the Tao, the flow, the effortless way of things. Tao also means ''just this much.''

Stephen Levine,
Who Dies?

LETTING GO

You have grown wings of pain
and flap around the bed like a wounded gull
calling for water, calling for tea, for grapes
whose skins you cannot penetrate.
Remember when you taught me
how to swim? Let go, you said,
the lake will hold you up.
I long to say, Father let go
and death will hold you up.
Outside the fall goes on without us.
How easily the leaves give in.
I hear them on the last breath of wind,
passing this disappearing place.

Linda Pastan,
''Go Gentle''

He searched for his accustomed fear of death and could not find it.

Leo Tolstoy,
The Death of Ivan Ilyich

BILL'S STORY

When my sister came back from Africa,
we didn't know at first how everything
had changed. After a while Annie
bought men's and boys' clothes in all sizes,
and filled her closets with little
or huge things she could never wear.

Then she took to buying out
theatrical shops, rental places on the skids,
sweeping in and saying, *I'll take everything.*
Dementia was the first sign of something
we didn't even have a name for,
in 1978. She was just becoming stranger

—all those clothes, the way she'd dress me up
when I came to visit. It was like we could go back
to playing together again, and get it right.
She was a performance artist, and she did
her best work then, taking the clothes to clubs,
talking, putting them all on, talking.

It was years before she was in the hospital,
and my mother needed something
to hold onto, some way to be helpful,
so she read a book called *Deathing*
(a cheap, ugly verb if ever I heard one)
and took its advice to heart;

she'd sit by the bed and say, *Annie,
look for the light, look for the light.*
It was plain that Anne did not wish

to be distracted by these instructions;
she came to, though she was nearly gone then,
and looked at our mother with what was almost
    certainly

annoyance. *It's a white light,*
Mom said, and this struck me
as incredibly presumptuous, as if the light
we'd all go into would be just the same.
Maybe she wanted to give herself up
to indigo, or red. If we can barely even speak

to each other, living so separately,
how can we all die the same?
I used to take the train to the hospital,
and sometimes the only empty seats
would be the ones that face backwards.
I'd sit there and watch where I'd been

waver and blur out, and finally
I liked it, seeing what you've left
get more beautiful, less specific.
Maybe her light was all that gabardine
and flannel, khaki and navy
and silks and stripes. If you take everything,

you've got to let everything go. Dying
must take more attention than I ever imagined.
Just when she'd compose herself
and seem fixed on the work before her,
Mother would fret, trying to help her
just one more time: *Look for the light,*

until I took her arm
and told her wherever I was in the world
I would come back, no matter how difficult
it was to reach her, if I heard her calling.
Shut up, mother, I said, and Annie died.

Mark Doty

Dying is a wild night and a new road.

Emily Dickinson

Coming Home

The following excerpts are from the book Conversations at Midnight *by Herbert and Kay Kramer. Herb, a former workaholic, is dying a slow enough death from prostate cancer that he has time to reflect on the process. His wife Kay brings to these "conversations" insights from her work doing therapy with dying people.*

Acknowledging Death

HERB: People will say, "Herb has such courage; he's putting up such a good fight." But I'm afraid that it is really more flight than fight, an attempt to distance myself from the process of dying, which I've already begun, though as yet, I have not felt a difference, physically or emotionally.

I suppose that everyone who approaches death has the same desire to flee, to create a diversion, to put up a battle, even though the battle might be a sham. I must know more about dying. . . .

KAY: Living, dying, and death are not divisible. The process Lewis Thomas writes about, the peace at the time of death, can be yours throughout the whole time of dying. The anguish, the fears, are not physical but psychological. They interfere with the natural process. They are not a part of it. Like prejudice or superstition, they've been learned, and they are not in harmony with natural experience. We're protected in dying by defenses that are born in us. But we need to get back in touch with them. We've lost so much of our self-awareness that we have to be reminded of what we've known all along. . . .

❧

Of course you feel that self-doubt now. You're still on the other side of the door, the tunnel, this dimension— whatever you call it. You have not begun to experience the transition. You have to understand that dying is a process of transition, from one state of being to another. In all the cases in which I've been involved with people who are aware of their dying, I've found a growing perception of death that the rest of us don't generally have. That is why they have so much to teach us. We learn from them. They are the experts who show us the way.

HERB: I have shunned making decisions about burial versus cremation, funeral or memorial service, ashes scattered in the Kramer Memorial Rose Garden at Cape Cod (four rose bushes surrounding a bird bath) or placed in the earth in Kay's family plot.

Nor have I tried to inform my adult children and step-children of any wishes I might have about their participation in whatever ceremonies mark the occasion of my passing. Is this passivity a natural response to the unthinkable, or part of my own bewilderment in the face of the unalterable? I have been the planner and orator at other funerals of family and friends. Should I be planning now how I should be memorialized?

KAY: Our instinct for survival is so strong, so deep-seated, that we defend ourselves against death by denying it. If we bring it to the surface in conversation with friends or loved ones, we're called morbid, depressing. . . . And when our elderly parents or grandparents try to bring our attention to fears, plans, or desires concerning their deaths, we tend to brush them off by saying, "Oh, come on, don't be so gloomy. You know you're going to outlive all of us." Or, we make a joke like, "Oh, Grandma, you're too mean to die." Or we say, "Not in front of the children, Dad. We'll talk about it later." Discussing death is a "no-no" in our culture. The American way of death is denial. Then, when it enters our lives, we try to make up for our neglect by buying the most expensive coffin, or arranging the most hurried, least-personal funeral service, just to get it behind us. . . . Other cultures are enriched by their recognition that death is central to life, not some intrusion that it's better not to think about. Death is un-American.

It doesn't square with our philosophy of optimism, of progress. Even our Declaration of Independence guarantees us "Life, Liberty, and the Pursuit of Happiness." Death is the great spoiler of all three, the ants at the picnic. We know life isn't like that at all, but our science, our industry, even our religion are geared toward an affirmation of life and a rejection of the reality of death. We can see this in the strange grief reaction this country had to the Gulf War. We ignored completely, felt nothing about, the deaths of hundreds of thousands of Iraqi soldiers and civilians. Only the fact that so few of our own soldiers died counted, and even they were largely ignored in the euphoria of our "quick and painless" victory. On the other hand, we seem to be anesthetized to death real and staged on television and in movies. I've read, for example, that the average American child witnesses eight thousand real deaths and thousands more staged deaths on television before the age of sixteen.

Unfinished Business

HERB: When my stepmother, Dora, began to have delusions in her late seventies, her mother would come to visit her every morning. She would be there when Dora awoke, lying on the twin bed where my father had slept throughout the twenty years of their marriage. No matter that she had died in 1927, she was very much there, and, according to Dora, they had the kind of long, intimate conversations they never were able to have in earlier times. The visits usually ended the same way. Her mother would ask for a cup of coffee, Dora would go into the kitchen to make it, and when she returned, her mother was gone.

Her father never came. Dora missed him; she had been his favorite, while her mother had doted on her feckless brother. When Dora told the story of the latest visitation in the presence of a psychiatrist, he simply said, "You must have a lot of unfinished business with your mother." It was the first time I had heard that term used to describe a relationship that had ended badly, in misunderstanding or anger.

Now, as I begin my own walk through the valley of the shadow, I am acutely conscious of the need to leave no unfinished business, to pay my debts, to reconnect with old friends, to write or telephone people whom I have long neglected (or who have neglected me). Like the toothache sufferer who keeps probing the cavity with his tongue, I probe my heart for incompleteness, and I experience daily the pain of fragmented relationships with two of my children, children now in their forties, who have chosen to distance themselves from me even as they have tightened their bonds with their brothers and sisters.

My impulse, of course, is to try to fix everything before my death. If nothing else, to let them know I feel only unconditional love for them and will, if they seek it, give them my blessing and my forgiveness. And then, I think, wait a minute! I am angry and hurt. Am I picturing some Dickensian scene of resolution around my death bed, when all wounds are healed, all hurts forgiven, and everyone walks away from the body guilt-free?

How important is it, in anticipation of death, to com-

plete all unfinished business? Is it my job to leave everyone feeling resolved and guilt-free? Did I learn more at
seventeen from my mother's hurt last letter than from
the inscription on her photograph, "To my son who has
never disappointed me," which I knew was a lie?!

. . . There are some relationships in my life that are
not what I would like them to be. My tendency and habit
are simply to say, "I forgive all," but I know that is the
coward's way out. On the other hand, I don't know if I
have the physical and emotional strength to attempt a
deeper therapeutic resolution. Is there a middle road between blanket pardon and the too-late, in-depth attempt
to work out so many tangled relationships in my family
that have gone on for so many years?

I've tried to paper over the cracks and the mildew and
pretend to myself and the world that "everything is
fine"—my favorite words. And now I'm afraid of having
waited until the last minute, when the only option left is
superficial forgiveness.

KAY: . . . Forgiveness can hardly be called superficial.
Forgiveness is one of the most powerful ideas in religion.
Injury and forgiveness. We seem to have an innate need
to make whole what is broken. Resolution is part of
forgiveness, a letting go, a surrender of hurt, of anger, of
grievance. But that's your work, to bring yourself to
resolution, not to say all the right words, make all the
right gestures, so that the death-bed scene will make
everyone feel good at the moment, without really healing
anything at all. . . .

I'm talking about honesty. This is what we've learned

from support groups. Health improves and life can be prolonged beyond expectation by participation in a group where people are free to express themselves openly and honestly, unbound by the "shoulds" of social convention. Statistically, such people go beyond those who are not connected to others in these positive ways. Giving ourselves permission to be more direct with others makes life less complicated. For you to batter yourself at a door that is closed would be unhealthy. Nor is it very satisfying when someone waits to be responsive to you in a positive way until you are near death and without the energy or desire to really interact with them. This intimate time is one that you may wish to spend among those who are truly able to love you without ambiguity.

The Grief Process

HERB: Because of this aversion to passionate, uncontrollable expression of high emotion, I have never resonated to Elisabeth Kübler-Ross's stages of grief and bereavement. I have never been able to be a part of mass grief or hysteria when tragedy strikes a public figure or the nation rejoices at the end of a war. And so, I am anesthetized against strong emotion concerning my own illness, just as I cannot conceive that my dying and my death will provoke strong feelings in those who apparently love me. . . .

I remember when Karyl [his first wife] had to be institutionalized at Hartford Hospital because she had tried to jump out of a moving automobile. It was one of the lowest, most desperate times in my life. Yet, as I was editing a speech at the office, standing next to my secretary's desk, I was totally unaware that I was whistling a pop tune. And at that moment, that desperate moment, my secretary said, "Mr. Kramer, you're the most cheerful person I have ever met." What should have been grief was the emotional blankness of denial, accompanied by a sound track of counterfeit feeling. Why have I such a difficult struggle giving myself over to the grief process? How and when does it begin? And if it can't begin, if it remains locked inside, how can there ever be understanding, acceptance, and resolution?

KAY: The grief process starts with an event, an event that, at first, seems incomprehensible, unmanageable. For you, the event is your dying. In response to the event, the grief process flows naturally and unimpeded to a resolution. That seems to be the way we are designed, like those pop-up toys you hit all the way to the floor, which then bounce right back up.

Some people get stuck or give up before the grief process has run its natural course. But left to run its course, it moves from stage to stage until there is spiritual, emotional, or intellectual resolution. Pathology is measured in terms of intensity and duration. How is the final resolution achieved?

. . . People who do poorly in grief resolution are those unable to find that context of meaning, a framework that creates sense and order out of the chaos of the event that triggers the grief process. It's like the prisoner in the camp who says, "My humanity is not something to be destroyed by someone else. I am going to live long enough to get out and tell my story."

For you, I will be there to help you let the process flow to allow meaning and growth to occur. But you have to unblock your deeply entrenched denial and let this healing, natural process begin to flow.

HERB: I find at this stage of the journey, I am much closer to the kind of naked emotion I have so often suppressed in the past, or not felt at all. I am angry that I have been treated so shabbily by my employers; I find tears just behind, if not in my eyes, when I remember a beautiful moment we've shared, like that magic day in the meadow. I experience black despair at the knowledge that this treatment, my last hope for more time, did not work, and I am going to be left weakened, compromised, vulnerable, an old, sick man on a cane. This seems an outrageous injustice. But then, I feel the old terror that strong emotion means loss of control, and I set out deliberately to tamp it down. I'm in touch with these feelings; I know they are there, but I can't seem to let them out.

KAY: When there is so much grief, it is sometimes very threatening to allow ourselves free expression of our fear, sadness, anger, and despair. We may be afraid that if we feel and express it, we will either go mad or become stuck in interminable agony. It may be hard to trust it as a natural process which, by its very nature, moves. It is necessary to have a safe place to express these deep feelings. And, if they are to be shared, it must be with others who understand and are not afraid or judgmental. I have experienced this safety with a few close friends, in therapy, and in therapy groups.

HERB: You speak of reaching out for support, the support of friends when you hit bottom. But I've never known or sought that kind of support. During so many dyings, I wouldn't have known whom to seek out, to whom to cry out, to be held, to be heard. Nor would I have wanted this support. I was in control and I guess I wanted it that way. You were safe. I was alone in the midst of danger, whistling, tying up all the loose ends, covering up grief with busy work. Why can't I reach out to others? Even to reach out to you, now, I find difficult.

KAY: I think you used the key word, *control.* It's hard to let go, particularly for a man. It makes me feel very sad that you have carried so much for so long. I am particularly moved by your finding it difficult even to reach out to me. I know what you mean. I am desperately trying to hold myself together, too, and you may sense this. I'm involved in my own grief process, and at times, I am unavailable. So, habit and individual need make this hard.

The Spiritual Journey

HERB: I had another dream a few days ago. Because of increasing edema caused by the Suramin, I lay on the couch with my legs elevated and fell asleep reading a book on transcendental meditation. In my almost-sleep state, I asked for a mantra, a phrase, syllables, that would help me with my meditating. When I was completely asleep, I dreamed that I was in Lhasa, in Tibet. The monks in their saffron robes were twirling the prayer wheels. There were pennants flying and the sound of unison chanting. I felt a great happiness, a sense of bliss, in Joseph Campbell's words. And then, my mantra came to me. It was, "Nothing dies." Now, wherever I am, whatever I am doing, when I repeat these words, I can see immediately the whirling prayer wheels, the flapping pennants, hear the chanting of the monks, and I feel again the great happiness first experienced in the dream. Is this a spiritual experience, a message from beyond myself, or am I simply trying desperately to disguise the reality of the final ending with a hope for heaven?

KAY: . . . Confronting your own death clears away a lot of tangled underbrush you've accumulated over the years. I sense that you are fully convinced that you have embarked on a new and deeper kind of journey, a journey that you accept on its own terms, not one that you have taken before. We must compensate for our unnatural fear of death with the reminder of the safety of the natural process.

HERB: If I could find some "context of meaning" in my dying, I guess I would have an easier time turning away from the mundane and focusing inward. Maybe that is still to come. But right now, I can't seem to get beyond my feeling of such unnecessary waste of a still-productive life because a careless, inefficient doctor missed the call until it was too late. Am I stuck in a part of the grief process that is inhibiting my spiritual development? Am I really asking the whining question I have always scorned, "Why me?" . . . How easy it has been to give up, to let go of work, achievement, goals, business, all the temporal activities and occupations that filled my life with activity, and essentially defined who I was to myself and the world. This is also true of the peripheral activities that once made up a "social life." I am sorry about this, because it means I am dragging you, too, into isolation and loneliness. But physical and psychic limitations have forced me into a state where I seem to want only peace, solitude, beauty, and a chance to reflect. In other words, a "garden." Even much of reading, of television, of keeping up with the world, has lost its power to illuminate, soothe, entertain, and distract. Am I entering a new stage of existence where, without realizing it, I am already on my spiritual journey through a whole new landscape of thought and feeling?

KAY: How much has it taken to shock you out of that high-speed world in which real events were all that counted; in which several newspapers had to be read every day; television news watched; radio's *All Things Considered* a must just at dinnertime. And then you had to think and talk about what you had read and listened to. Ideas. Ideas. Ideas. Never time for quiet reflection. Life was too full, too crowded with deadlines, assignments, and challenges. . . .

Remember that the object of all spiritual life that incorporates celibacy is to rid oneself of the sexual drive, to refocus this energy on the love of God with all one's being. The loss of sexual capacity has functioned for you in some ways. It has been good for me in some ways, too, as it has made you such an easier person to live with. You are less driven and more accepting.

The loss of sexual activity which played such a strong part in our relationship has been devastating to me. I ask myself if I will ever be in a sexual relationship again. I feel that I am dying, too, that my sexual life is dead. This may not be true, but it feels like it. My anger is expressed in a kind of turning off. It doesn't function the same for me as for you, because I don't have the disease. It's why I have put on weight, eaten the wrong foods to satisfy myself physically. Food has taken the place of sex.

The Power of Love

HERB: So much has happened emotionally that I feel quite different now from the way I felt several months ago. It is as if I have undergone a spring thaw, melting and cracking the ice that has held my deepest emotions immobilized, frozen—emotions that seem to be a part of a process that is the opposite of the full range of the process of grieving. It has resulted in an overwhelming rush of warmth, empathy, and caring that embraces everyone, everything. It's like the song (and we all know the power of cheap music) that goes, ''There's a smile on my face for the whole human race, why it's almost like being in love.'' Even the tears that I shed, and they come frequently, are not tears of grief or frustration, but the satisfying tears that accompany genuine feeling. Have you ever experienced this phenomenon in other dying patients or clients? What is it? How does it function for me at this stage of the process?

KAY: It always seems amazing to find that there are things to be gained in the midst of such hideous loss. That is why some people who have had cancer say that the disease is the best thing that ever happened to them. These are called secondary gains. In therapy, we try to discover what the disease is enabling people to do so that they might be able to achieve the same goals without needing the disease. We attempt to find ways of accomplishing those ends at a less drastic cost. We don't want to need the disease.

HERB: And so the end of the grief process, too, is the discovery that love overcomes loss, and the final reconciliation is with the fact that, as I dreamed when I asked my Tibetan monks for a mantra, it was—"Nothing dies."

KAY: Yes.

Home, Hospital, Hospice

HERB: Now, August 1991, earlier on the very day I am writing this, I have been told bluntly but kindly that all hormone therapy has failed and that I have only a few months to live. This gives great importance, if not urgency, to the subject of the surroundings of my final dying and my death. Having no direct experience of the hospice concept, I know it only from what I have read and what Kay has told me about it. I appreciate its attention to the alleviation of pain and to the creation of an affirming, sustaining environment in the days of final transition. My fear is, however, that its finality, if one is aware of it, signals the death of all hope, all options to live. . . .

I feel that the issue of where I'm going to die is as important to me right now as when I'm going to die. Unless some quick and lethal pneumonia or stroke carries me off unexpectedly, I'm assuming that the disease will maintain a relatively slow, downhill course, permitting me the luxury (if it can be called that) of a choice of where to die. . . .

I would like, at the end, to be able to see the tree outside the bedroom window, to sit or lie on the flower-filled sun porch, and, whatever the season, to look out on the garden with its statue of calm, serene Buddha at its center. I would like to have Kay near, to enjoy the last quiet moments with my dog and cat, to feel that children and friends, if they wanted to visit, could come to the place of beauty that Kay, with a little bit of me, had shaped. . . .

KAY: Where to die? I think of the deathbed scenes in books and movies from prehospital death times. The central focus of these scenes is the massive bed, the dying one propped up with lots of pillows; the soft glow of candlelight creating an aura of holiness; the chamber filled with solemn, praying people, loved ones ministering to the needs of the one who is dying; friends and acquaintances lined up for final farewells; and relatives eager to hear the last words and to witness the passage of the soul into heaven. This sacred place near the one who is becoming holy because of proximity to the great mystery is a far cry from what I found when I began my training as a chaplain in the general hospital setting. Consigned to a place where success was measured by medical cure, the dying ones were hidden as if a failure and an embarrassment. . . . This is what motivated me to go into social work. It seemed simple to me. I thought, *What do I want for me and those I love when our time to die comes?* It was not this abandonment and inhumane neglect.

It is essential for you to know that whatever the choice—it's yours to make. You are not going to be sent away to a residential hospice or a hospital or kept at home against your will.

. . . The main benefit of hospice is that death is not considered a failure. It is a natural event to be lived through in a spirit of grace. And not only does it care for the needs of its patients and their families—until the moment of death—it then helps the family process its grief, handle its bereavement, and reflect on the entire mysterious and beautiful experience.

Letting Go

HERB: At work, I had been fighting to remain employed until I reach seventy, a promise to me which had been made and broken. My employers wanted me to continue to meet their needs at a greatly reduced salary and no benefits. "We just don't have the money," they said.

So . . . I must let the idea of "letting go" penetrate my defenses and bring me to a place where I can no longer be defined by my work, my energy, my ability, my pride, my ego. I must let go of the phantoms of service, of accomplishment, and of self-importance that have pursued me for almost fifty years. . . .

Obviously, I have "let go," because either consciously or unconsciously, I no longer have the will or the strength to keep going as I was before. But letting go has not been the traumatic experience I thought it would be. I don't have a sense of struggling to maintain some status in the world of affairs. Nor do I feel that if I do let go, I'll drop into a black hole. I do have a sense of dropping into an unfamiliar but comfortable world of reflection, quiet, and rediscovery. . . .

With the expectation of a few months of life, I'm aware that everything—from the turning of the seasons, to holidays, birthdays, and special occasions, is probably for me, a last-time experience. This makes everything more pregnant with meaning. Yet it also fosters the awareness that, one page at a time, I am letting go of life itself. To know that this is the last Thanksgiving, the last Christmas, the last novels by Anne Tyler or Robertson Davies, the last trip on a plane, is both depressing and strangely seductive. Since this awareness heightens the real and symbolic significance of every such experience, should I be closing doors, one by one, bowing to those who have set my sentence? If I pretend that everything is normal and, of course, will be repeated in the next cycle of seasons and occasions, does this not rob me of the chance to extract every ounce of sweetness from these experiences—knowing they will not be repeated?

. . . The day I learned that there was little or no hope of slowing down the march of the cancer medically, my 1991 calendar and appointment book dropped and fell apart. As I tried to reassemble the pages, and as I reviewed the constant activity that characterized my days until now, I realized with much pain and guilt how trivial most of this activity was. The writing of this book is an essential part of "letting go," so that I can fully experience this new stage of my life and make reparation to you for my failure to put first things first—before they became "last things." How can I find other forms of mental or spiritual activity, other strategies for making this time a richer, more productive experience?

The awareness of "last things" makes them seem more precious and poignant, but their loss does not seem to bring as much grief as I thought it would. I do want to hold on to what I have, whom and what I love—but I realize that I must be willing to "let go" before I can truly "come home" through the portal of death. I know this seems self-centered, even cold, but it seems to be part of a natural process that is beyond reason or control.

Thanks to our "Conversations at Midnight," whispered in intimacy when we were together, or taking the form of telephone calls and written dialogue during the weeks we were apart, I have changed in strange and unexpected ways since our dialogue began. My fears of dying and death have been resolved. My feelings of loss and bereavement have been almost neutralized by a sense of joy and wonder in the knowledge that I am not moving toward oblivion but, rather, that I am "coming home." I am not even sure I know what "coming home" means.

But I am certain in my deepest being, that I have begun a new and unexpectedly exciting and beautiful part of the journey back to the source, to the mystery from which I emerged into this life seventy years ago.

Gone is the terror that my unique, individual consciousness may come to an end; gone is the egocentric need to affirm the continuity of myself. I seem to live now surrounded by a ring of light whose source I cannot decipher. The poignancy of pumpkins, of fall foliage, of holidays, of music and poetry are still precious, but no longer the indispensable furniture of home.

> Herbert Kramer and
> Kay Kramer,
> edited excerpts from
> *Conversations at Midnight*

Death has dominion because it is not only the start of nothing but the end of everything, and how we think and talk about dying—the emphasis we put on dying with "dignity"—shows how important it is that life ends *appropriately,* that death keeps faith with the way we want to have lived.

> Ronald Dworkin

Sunset and evening star,
   And one clear call for me!
And may there be no moaning of the bar,
   When I put out to sea,

But such a tide as moving seems asleep,
  Too full for sound and foam.
When that which drew from out the boundless deep
  Turns again home.

Twilight and evening bell,
  And after that the dark!
And may there be no sadness of farewell,
  When I embark;

For though from out our bourne of Time and Place
  The flood may bear me far,
I hope to see my Pilot face to face
  When I have crost the bar.

Alfred, Lord Tennyson,
from "Crossing the Bar"

I have got my leave. Bid me farewell, my brothers! I bow
to you all and take my departure.

Here I give back the keys of my door—and I give up
all claims to my house. I only ask for last kind words
from you.

We were neighbors for long, but I received more than
I could give. Now the day has dawned and the lamp that
lit my dark corner is out. A summons has come and I am
ready for my journey.

Rabindranath Tagore,
from *Gitanjali*

Let it not be death but completeness.

Let love melt into memory and pain into songs.

Let the flight through the sky end in the folding of the wings over the nest.

Let the last touch of your hands be gentle like the flower of the night.

Stand still, O Beautiful End, for a moment, and say your last words in silence.

I bow to you and hold up my lamp to light you on your way.

                    Rabindranath Tagore

SAYING

GOOD-BYE

In the face of death we can discriminate between the important and the trivial. We sometimes drop our habitual or guardian reticence and speak clearly.

Lewis Hyde,
The Gift

A Dying Man Clears Up Unfinished Business

Looking back with love, I know that my father was never what you'd call a role model. A peripatetic safety engineer, for much of his life he was a very self-centered man, loud and gruff, with a wide circle of acquaintances, an impressive number of professional accomplishments, but few close friends. Four times divorced, he lived his life on his own terms, for the most part excluding his four children until we were adults ourselves. His relationship with his two sons and two daughters was marked by periods of closeness and estrangement, not an uncommon story in a country where family members often live hundreds of miles from one another, where family ties are unfortunately easier to break than to strengthen.

What makes our story different is what happened when this flawed man found out that he had only three months to live. It would have been easy for my father to be selfish in the last days allotted to him. Instead, he met his death with courage, spirit and—perhaps most amazing of all—a thoughtfulness for those he would leave behind that he had rarely demonstrated throughout his life. He set the tone for dealing with our fear and his own, and in doing so he forged a new and enduring family bond. . . .

In his last soul-searching months, he replaced his selfishness with a burning desire to tie up emotional loose ends with his children—the offspring from three different marriages. (He had long ago burned his bridges with his four ex-wives and did not try to contact them now.) He wanted to understand more about the effects of his behavior on his children, and he sought counseling to deal with his unresolved conflicts with each of us.

Perhaps the greatest gift he gave to us, and we to him, was the family reunion. He picked a date in early January—a month after some of his doctors predicted he'd be dead (they had told him he had two to three months, and he chose to believe the longer span)—and arranged for us to be together for four days in California for a last visit. At one point in early December he began to fail and panicked, wanting to move up the date. But the four of us consulted over the phone and decided that we'd stand firm if he'd fight to stay alive for one more Christmas, to beat the odds for a few more weeks. He rallied.

The week before the reunion, my father called each of

us. "Now I want you to think of *any* question that you might have about our family or me or my life," he said. "I'll tell you anything you want to know." He wanted us to understand, to be fearless in our curiosity, as he was trying to be fearless with his answers. . . .

When I arrived in Sacramento, Dennis picked me up at the airport and we went out for a drink before visiting our father. "I want to prepare you for what you will see," he said. I'm glad that he did. For the robust man I had seen a year before was no more. In his place was a painfully thin, frail man who seemed to have aged a hundred years, someone who could sit up for only a few minutes at a time, whose mobility was hampered by an oxygen tank and who seemed to be just hanging on with every ounce of his failing energy.

His spirit was still there—there were lists on the refrigerator, a schedule of events, dinners and private time allotted for each of us. But the look in his eyes was different from the untrammeled bravado I remembered, replaced by a vulnerability, an acceptance and a painful desire to right all the wrongs in the time left. He was seeking redemption and our understanding, and his near-heroic efforts to beat back the exhaustion and physical ruin of his present circumstances touched each of us deeply.

The four days went by in an exhausting haze. We'd visit with Dad until he had to go back to bed, then the four of us would go out together, sampling restaurants, taking long walks, pitching in together to help around the house, fielding phone calls from Dad's friends, monitoring each other's spirits—for we each, in our own ways, were afraid, too. We not only grew closer with our father, we also became closer as siblings, sharing our feelings every step of the way.

On our first night together, after Dad had gone to sleep, we went to a local bar for margaritas—a tradition whenever we were together. Practically at the same time, we all voiced what we had individually been worrying about: When Dad dies, does it mean we won't be a family anymore? We laughed that we all had come to Sacramento with the same worry, then vowed to be even closer—geography be damned—after Dad died.

I had brought my tape recorder and several blank tapes for my private sessions with Dad. True to his nature of thinking of everything, he had borrowed a better one, with blank tapes and extra batteries for all. Each of us went in alone to talk to Dad in those last days—an hour here, an hour there. We took turns and made sure each person had equal time, adhering to Dad's schedule as much as possible.

I took my father at his word, asking him the questions I had been too angry or shy or self-centered to ask through all the years. Drinking whiskey and soda and chain-smoking—after all, he knew he was dying, so why shouldn't he enjoy his last days?—he laughed and cried with me, reaching out in a frank and loving way that I had always wanted but that it took impending death to accomplish.

At times I could see his fear, and I hugged him, trying to be a source of strength. Then he'd pick up the thread of our talk and plunge in with as much detail as he could remember. Family history, genealogy, his relationship with his mother and father, his experiences in the war— we covered them all. His divorce from my mother, the guilt he felt at not being around in my formative years, how he had wanted to change, how badly he felt about not being the kind of father the textbooks say he should have been.

At the end of our sessions, my father would fall asleep and I'd go into the living room. My sister and brothers were there and would give me hugs and buck me up. When they each had their turns, I and the other two would do the same. (I have three hours of my father's voice on tape still, as does each of my siblings.)

On the last day, in the living room, jokes and smiles reigned: we wanted to keep these last precious moments of normalcy as bright as possible. When the sadness hit, we would go into a corner Dad couldn't see to hug one another until it passed. We brought out the cameras for pictures: Dad with his children, Dad with his grandchildren, Dad with his sons and with his daughters, a group shot of everyone crowded on the couch. Every possible combination.

Too soon it was time for me to leave. "You're going on a wonderful adventure," I said as I hugged my father for the last time. We were both crying, and he thanked me over and over for coming. I thought of the first thing that might cheer him up: "Just think, you'll meet Thomas Jefferson and finally discover what really happened to Judge Crater. And when you do, I want you to come back and tell me all about it." He hugged me tighter. "I will"—he smiled—"I will."

Mary Alice Kellogg,
"Good-bye, Dad . . . and
Thanks"

SAYING GOOD-BYE

There are many ways to say good-bye, and all of them are good. Maybe even like death, they are perfect.

Several charities such as the Starlight Foundation and the Make-A-Wish Foundation grant wishes to children with life-threatening diseases. These very ill children, some of whom may be terminal, and their families are the guests of the host charity who is granting the wish. One of the most popular wishes is a trip to Disney World. This fun-filled vacation may be the last experience that the family has together away from the hospital; it gives the child and the family a happy image to remember during the difficult time ahead. After the child is gone, it remains a cherished memory.

While this is not a formal closing, it can be a step in the closing process. When my best friend was dying and while he could still get around, we took a vacation and looked back on the years of our friendship. Today, that's one of my strongest memories of him, rather than the darker days of his passing.

The first time I witnessed a closing, and long before I heard it called that, was in the movie *Harold and Maude*.

The film is about a vital old woman, Maude, played by Ruth Gordon, who has a love affair with a morose young boy, Harold, played by Bud Cort. They both enjoy funerals, and that is where they meet.

In one of the most touching scenes, the two sit on the shore of a lake. Harold gives Maude a coin from a carnival machine with "Harold loves Maude" engraved on it. Maude holds the coin for a moment against her heart and then tosses it into the water. Harold is bewildered by her gesture, but then Maude turns to him and says: "So I'll always know where it is."

The film is about how Maude gives Harold the spirit and joy of life while she gets ready for her death. And when she dies, they both are ready, even though Harold wants her to go on living. In the final scene we witness Maude's triumph as Harold embraces life on his own.

Saying good-bye can be a joy.

As death approaches we do not need to turn away in fear. Instead we can choose to celebrate life and join hands with those we love. We can sing and dance and make merry in the face of the lengthening shadow. We can take the time that remains to add a few magical moments to our book of memories. And when twilight falls and the moon rises and the one we love passes from us, we can take solace in the knowledge that we embraced and said good-bye.

When it was clear that Dave was going to die, he and Joan began a beautiful closing. They loved one another very much and had not had much time together before

Dave became sick. To all of us who knew them, their love seemed like a miracle because they had both been looking for a partner for a long time.

The idea that Dave was going to leave us was too terrible to consider. The closing they planned for us was one of the kindest and most gentle that I know.

We each received a letter inviting us to a garden party for Dave. We were to bring a plant that would be placed in Dave's garden among all his favorite plants—his plants and ours growing side by side in a friendly memory.

Now, after Dave is gone, Joan can sit in his garden and remember the sunny day when friends joined together to say good-bye. She can tend Dave's garden as she tended him, with love and devotion. Together they planted a living, growing memory, bright and beautiful and sweet with the fragrance of life.

> Ted Menten,
> *Gentle Closings*

See also GRIEF RITUALS, page 293.

And After Death—What?

THE NEAR-DEATH EXPERIENCE

We have become very familiar now in the West with the near-death experience, the name given to the range of experiences reported by people who have survived an incident of near or clinical death. The near-death experience has been reported throughout history, in all mystical and shamanic traditions, and by writers and philosophers as varied as Plato, Pope Gregory the Great, some of the great Sufi masters, Tolstoy, and Jung.

The skill of modern medical technology has added a new and exciting dimension to the extent of the near-death experience: many people have now been revived from "death," for example, after accidents, heart attack, or serious illness, or in operations or combat. The near-death experience has been the subject of a great deal of scientific research and philosophical speculation. According to an authoritative 1982 Gallup poll, an extraordinary number of Americans—up to 8 million, or one in twenty in the population—have had at least one near-death experience.

Although no two people have exactly the same experience . . . a common pattern of different phases in the near-death experience, a "core experience," appears:

• They experience an altered state of feeling, of peace and well-being, without pain, bodily sensations, or fear.

• They may be aware of a buzzing or rushing sound, and find themselves separated from their body. This is the so-called "out-of-the-body experience": They can view the body, often from a point somewhere above it; their sense of sight and hearing is heightened; their consciousness is clear and vividly alert, and they can even move through walls.

• They are aware of another reality, of entering a darkness, floating in a dimensionless space, and then moving rapidly through a tunnel.

• They see a light, at first a point in the distance, and are magnetically drawn toward it and then enveloped in light and love. This light is described as a blinding light of great beauty, but the eyes are unhurt by it. Some people report meeting "a being of light," a luminous, seemingly omniscient presence that a few call God or Christ, who is compassionate and loving. Sometimes in this presence they may witness a life-review, seeing everything they have done in their life, good and bad. They communicate telepathically with the presence, and find themselves in a timeless and usually blissful dimension in which all ordinary concepts like time and space are meaningless. Even if the experience lasts only one or two minutes in normal time, it can be of a vast elaboration and richness.

• Some see an inner world of preternatural beauty, paradisal landscapes and buildings, with heavenly music, and they have a feeling of oneness. A very few, it seems, report terrifying visions of hellish realms.

• They may reach a boundary beyond which they cannot go; some meet dead relatives and friends and talk to them. They decide (often reluctantly) or are told to return to the body and this life, sometimes with a sense of mission and service, sometimes to protect and care for their family, sometimes simply to fulfill the purpose of their life, which has not been accomplished.

The most important aspect of the near-death experience, as reported again and again in the literature about it, is the complete transformation it often makes in the lives, attitudes, careers, and relationships of the people who have this experience. They may not lose their fear of pain and dying, but they lose their fear of death itself: they become more tolerant and loving; and they become interested in spiritual values, the "path of wisdom," and usually in a universal spirituality rather than the dogma of any one religion.

One of the best descriptions of the approach to the light was reported by Margot Grey:

> Then gradually you realize that way, far off in the distance, an unmeasurable distance, you may be reaching the end of the tunnel, as you can see a white light, but it's so far away I can only compare it to looking up into the sky and in the distance seeing a single star, but visually you must remember that you are looking through a tunnel, and this light would fill

the end of the tunnel. You concentrate on this speck of light because as you are propelled forward you anticipate reaching this light.

Gradually, as you travel towards it at an extreme speed it gets larger and larger. The whole process on reflection only seems to take about one minute. As you gradually draw nearer to this extremely brilliant light there is no sensation of an abrupt end of the tunnel, but rather more of a merging into the light. By now, the tunnel is behind you and before you is this magnificent, beautiful blue-white light. The brilliance is so bright, brighter than a light that would immediately blind you, but absolutely does not hurt your eyes at all.

Another man who reached this point of entering the light describes it in this way:

> The following series of events appear to happen simultaneously, but in describing them I will have to take them one at a time. The sensation is of a being of some kind, more a kind of energy, not a character in the sense of another person, but an intelligence with whom it is possible to communicate. Also, in size it just covers the entire vista before you. It totally engulfs everything, you feel enveloped.
>
> The light immediately communicates to you, in an instant telekinesis your thought waves are read, regardless of language. A doubtful statement would be impossible to receive. The first message I received

was "Relax, everything is beautiful, everything is OK, you have nothing to fear." I was immediately put at absolute ease. In the past if someone like a doctor had said "It's OK, you have nothing to fear, this won't hurt," it usually did—you couldn't trust them.

But this was the most beautiful feeling I have ever known, it's absolute pure love. Every feeling, every emotion is just perfect. You feel warm, but it has nothing to do with temperature. Everything there is absolutely vivid and clear. What the light communicates to you is a feeling of true, pure love. You experience this for the first time ever. You can't compare it to the love of your wife, or the love of your children or sexual love. Even if all those things were combined, you cannot compare it to the feeling you get from this light.

Sogyal Rinpoche,
The Tibetan Book of Living and Dying

VIEWS OF IMMORTALITY

Death destroys the body, as the scaffolding is destroyed after the building is up and finished. And he whose building is up rejoices at the destruction of the scaffolding and of the body.

Leo Tolstoy

The tomb is not a blind alley; it is a thoroughfare. It closes on the twilight. It opens on the dawn.

Victor Hugo

Life is a constant sunrise, which death cannot interrupt, any more than the night can swallow up the sun.

George MacDonald,
Annals of a Quiet Neighborhood

Nothing dies; death and birth are but a threshold crossing, back and forth, as it were, through a veil.

Joseph Campbell

Has the body a soul? No. The soul has a body. And well does that soul know when this body has served its purpose, and well does that soul do to lay it aside in high austerity, taking it off like a stained garment.

Lucien Price,
Litany for All Souls

Only when you drink from the river of
silence shall you indeed sing.
And when you have reached the mountain
top, then you shall begin to climb.

And when the earth shall claim your
limbs, then shall you truly dance.

> Kahlil Gibran,
> from *The Prophet*

Here begins the open sea. Here begins the glorious adventure, the only one abreast with human curiosity, the
only one that soars as high as its highest longing. Let us
accustom ourselves to regard death as a form of life
which we do not yet understand; let us learn to look
upon it with the same eye that looks upon birth;
and soon our mind will be accompanied to the steps
of the tomb with the same glad expectation as greets a
birth.

> Maurice Maeterlinck,
> *Our Eternity*

People sleep, and when they die, they awake.

> Muhammad

Out of the finite darkness,
Into the infinite light.

> Louise Chandler Moulton

Those who practice Sufism, the mystical path of Islam, believe that we are already in immortality, and that the only changes to expect are the transition into your body (known as birth) and the transition out of it (known as death).

On that fatal day when my casket rolls along,
don't think my heart is in this world.
Don't cry, don't wail in anguish;
don't fall into a hole the demons have dug.
That surely would be sad.

When you see my procession, don't say I'm gone.
It will be my reunion.
As you lower me into the grave, don't say, "So long."
The grave is a veil before the gathering of paradise.

When you see that lowering down,
think of rising.

What harm is in the setting moon or sun?
What seems a setting to you is a dawning.

Though it may seem a prison,
this vault releases the soul.
Unless a seed enters the earth, it doesn't grow.
Why are you doubting this human seed?
Unless the bucket goes down,
it won't come up full.
Why should the Joseph of the Spirit resent the well?

Close your mouth here and open it beyond,
and in the nowhere air will be your song.

> Jelaluddin Rumi,
> "The Grave Is a Veil,"
> in *Love Is a Stranger*

For dust thou art, and unto dust shalt thou return.

> Genesis 3:19

I would like to believe when I die that I have given myself
away like a tree that sows seeds every spring and never
counts the loss, because it is not loss, it is adding to
future life. It is the tree's way of being. Strongly rooted
perhaps, but spilling out its treasure on the wind.

> May Sarton,
> *Recovering*

Verily, verily, I say unto you, Except a corn of wheat fall
into the ground and die, it abideth alone; but if it die, it
bringeth forth much fruit.

> John 12:24

I never saw a moor,
I never saw the sea:
Yet know I how the heather looks
And what a wave must be.

I never spoke with God,
Nor visited in heaven:
Yet certain am I of the spot
As if the chart were given.

Emily Dickinson

Because I could not stop for Death—
He kindly stopped for me—
The Carriage held but just Ourselves—
And Immortality.

We slowly drove—He knew no haste
And I had put away
My labour and my leisure too,
For His Civility—

We passed the School, where Children strove
At Recess—in the Ring—
We passed the Fields of Gazing Grain—
We passed the Setting Sun—

Or rather—He passed Us—
The Dews drew quivering and chill—
For only Gossamer, my Gown—
My Tippet—only Tulle—

We paused before a House that seemed
A Swelling of the Ground—
The Roof was scarcely visible—
The Cornice—in the Ground—

Since then—'tis Centuries—and yet
Feels shorter than the Day
I first surmised the Horses' Heads
Were toward Eternity—

Emily Dickinson

The door of death is made of gold,
That mortal eyes cannot behold;
But, when the mortal eyes are closed,
And cold and pale the limbs reposed,
The soul awakes; and wondering, sees
In her mild hand the golden keys . . .

William Blake

What is dying? I am standing on the sea shore. A ship sails to the morning breeze and starts for the ocean. She is an object of beauty and I stand watching her till at last she fades on the horizon, and someone at my side says, "She is gone." Gone where? Gone from my sight, that is all; she is just as large in the masts, hull and spars as she was when I saw her, and just as able to bear her load of living freight to its destination.

The diminished size and total loss of sight is in me, not

in her; and just at the moment when someone at my side says, "She is gone," there are others who are watching her coming, and other voices take up a glad shout, "There she comes"—and that is dying.

Bishop Brent

We cannot suppose that death is the stuff of any adventure except that of the body. . . . There will be things yet to be done, and the stuff that we work in will be the utterly familiar and still mysterious and exciting stuff of ourselves.

Mary Hunter Austin,
Experiences Facing Death

I have never seen, and never shall see, that the cessation of the evidence of existence is, necessarily, evidence of the cessation of existence.

William F. De Morgan

I make no pretence to knowing Who or What God is; but I am sure that we all owe our existence to something much higher than a passing moment of sexual ecstasy between our parents. I find it impossible to believe that creatures so complex as every one of us is could have been called into being for such a short span as is granted even to those who have the doubtful privilege of living longest. I can no more imagine Death as being final than I can imagine Space ending in a brick wall, or in a sort of celestial knacker's* yard.

> Lord Ballantrae,
> Chancellor of the University of
> St. Andrews, in a sermon
> shortly before his death, quoted
> in *All in the End Is Harvest*

* A knacker buys worn-out domestic livestock, such as a horse, and sells its products (to a glue factory, for example).

Is life the incurable disease?
The infant is born howling
& we laugh,
the dead man smiles
& we cry,
resisting the passage,
always resisting the passage,
that turns life
into eternity.

Blake sang alleluias
on his deathbed.
My own grandmother,
hardly a poet at all,
smiled
as we'd never seen her smile
before.
Perhaps the dress of flesh
is no more than a familiar garment

that grows looser as one diets
on death, & perhaps we discard it
or give it to the poor in spirit,
who have not learned yet
what blessing it is
to go naked?

> Erica Jong,
> "Is Life the Incurable
> Disease?"

For if a man should dream of heaven and, waking, find within his hand a flower as token that he had really been there . . . what then?

> Thomas Wolfe

We sometimes congratulate ourselves at the moment of waking from a troubled dream; it may be so the moment after death.

> Nathaniel Hawthorne

Birth must seem to the new-born babe what death seems to us—the annihilation of all the conditions which had hitherto made life possible in the womb of its mother, but proved to be its emergence into a wider life.

> Gustave Fechner,
> *Life After Death*

I believe that man will not merely endure; he will prevail. He is immortal, not because he alone among creatures has an inexhaustible voice, but because he has a soul, a spirit capable of compassion and sacrifice and endurance.

> William Faulkner,
> Nobel Prize acceptance speech,
> 1950

Death, be not proud, though some have called thee
Mighty and dreadful, for thou art not so;
For those whom thou think'st thou dost overthrow
Die not, poor Death, nor yet canst thou kill me.
From rest and sleep, which but thy pictures be,
Much pleasure, then from thee much more must flow;
And soonest our best men with thee do go—
Rest of their bones, and soul's delivery!
Thou'rt slave to fate, chance, kings, and desperate
    men,
And dost with poison, war, and sickness dwell;
And poppy or charms can make us sleep as well
And better than thy stroke. Why swell'st thou then?
One short sleep past, we wake eternally,
And Death shall be no more: Death, thou shalt die!

> John Donne,
> "Death Be Not Proud"

Prayers in

Many Voices

From too much love of living,
From hope and fear set free,
We thank with brief thanksgiving
Whatever gods may be
That no life lives for ever;
That dead men rise up never;
That even the weariest river
Winds somewhere safe to sea.

Algernon Charles Swinburne

The Lord is my shepherd; I shall not want.
He maketh me to lie down in green pastures:
He leadeth me beside the still waters.
He restoreth my soul:
He leadeth me in the paths of righteousness
for his name's sake.
Yea, though I walk through the valley of the
shadow of death, I will fear no evil:
For thou art with me: thy rod and thy staff
they comfort me.
Thou preparest a table before me in the presence
of mine enemies:
Thou anointest my head with oil; my cup runneth over.

Surely goodness and mercy shall follow me all
  the days of my life:
And I will dwell in the house of the Lord
  for ever.

> Psalm 23

Rest and peace eternal give them,
Lord Our God; and light for
evermore shine down upon them.

> Giuseppi Verdi

There is time of weeping and there is time of laughing.
But as you see, he setteth the weeping time before, for
that is the time of this wretched world and the laughing
time shall come after in heaven. There is also a time of
sowing, and a time of reaping too. Now must we in this
world sow, that we may in the other world reap: and in
this short sowing time of this weeping world, must we
water our seed with the showers of our tears, and then
shall we have in heaven a merry laughing harvest for ever.

> Sir Thomas More

Keep me in thy love
As thou wouldest that all should be kept in mine.
May everything in this my being
Be directed to thy glory
And may I never despair.

For I am under thy hand,
And in thee is all power and goodness.

Dag Hammarskjöld

Oh God,
Give me the courage to change the
things I can change,
the serenity to accept that which I
cannot change,
and the wisdom to distinguish between
the two.

Thomas C. Hart,
"The Serenity Prayer"

He did not say: You will not be troubled, you will not be
belabored, you will not be afflicted; but he said: You will
not be overcome.

Mother Julian of Norwich

When you pass through the waters,
I will be with you;
and when you pass through the rivers,
they will not sweep over you.

When you walk through the fire,
   you will not be burned;
      the flames will not set you ablaze.

Do not be afraid, for I am with you.

        Isaiah 43:2,5

To every thing there is a season, and a
   time to every purpose under the heaven:
A time to be born, and a time to die;
A time to plant, and a time to pluck up
   that which is planted;
A time to kill, and a time to heal;
A time to break down, and a time to build up;
A time to weep, and a time to laugh;
A time to mourn, and a time to dance.

        Ecclesiastes 3:1–4

Ample make this Bed—
Make this Bed with Awe—
In it wait till Judgment break
Excellent and Fair.

Be its Mattress straight—
Be its Pillow round—
Let no Sunrise' yellow noise
Interrupt this Ground—

        Emily Dickinson

I have no other helper than you, no other father, I pray
   to you.
Only you can help me. My present misery is too great.
Despair grips me, and I am at my wit's end.
O Lord, Creator, Ruler of the World, Father.
I thank you that you have brought me through.

How strong the pain was—but you were stronger.
How deep the fall was—but you were even deeper.
How dark the night was—but you were the noonday
   sun in it.
You are our father, our mother, our brother, and our
   friend.

An African's Prayer

Teach me your mood, o patient stars;
Who climb each night the ancient sky,
Leaving on space no shade, no scars,
No trace of age, no fear to die.

Ralph Waldo Emerson

Abide with me; fast falls the eventide;
   The darkness deepens; Lord, with me abide;
When other helpers fail, and comforts flee,
   Help of the helpless, O, abide with me.

Henry Francis Lyte

Dear Lord, be good to me.
Your sea is so wide and my boat is so small.

The Mariners' Prayer

May we all find peace in the shared hope that our children who brought us such joy with their short lives are now a host of angels, loving us still, feeling our love for them, awaiting our coming, and knowing that they are safely locked forever in our hearts.

Gordon Livingston,
Only Spring: On Mourning the Death of My Son

They shall not grow old, as we that are left grow old:
Age shall not weary them nor the years condemn.
At the going down of the sun, and in the morning,
We will remember them.

Laurence Binyon

Prayer for the Little Daughter
Between Death and Burial

Now you are standing face to face with the clear light
believe in it
Now you have gone back into where air comes from
hold fast to it
Now you have climbed to the top of the topless tower
and there are no stairs down
and the only way is flight past the edge of the world
do not remember us

Like the new moon in the sky of the shortest day
you came to us
as the candles burnt with a steady light behind misty
    windows
you whispered to us
as the singers moved behind doors of un-attainable
    rooms
you burst in on us
Lady of the shortest day, silent upon the threshold
carrying green branches

Lady of the crown of light going into clear light
be safe on your journey
Bright lady of the dark day, who pushed back the
    darkness
say nothing to us
as we plod through the frozen field
going from somewhere to somewhere
do not speak to us
as we stand at the centre of the frozen lake

and trees of cloud stand over us
forget us

When we come to you we shall find you
who have seen Persephone
you whom our mothers called Lady of the city
will welcome us with tapers, and believe in us
When small harsh birds bubble and pump in our nude
   trees
and water will rush and gush through the slippery
   street
and two skies will look at each other
one of air and one below
of water
you will rest with us, and of us:

Lady of the shortest day
watch over our daughter
whom we commit to the grass

Miriam Diana Scott,
in *Bread and Roses*

We Remember Them

In the rising of the sun and in its going down,
We remember them;

In the blowing of the wind and in the chill of winter,
We remember them;

In the opening of the buds and in the warmth of
summer,
We remember them;

In the rustling of leaves and the beauty of autumn,
We remember them;

In the beginning of the year and when it ends,
We remember them;

When we are weary and in need of strength,
We remember them;

When we are lost and sick at heart,
We remember them;

When we have joys we yearn to share,
We remember them;

So long as we live, they too shall live,
for they are now a part of us as

WE REMEMBER THEM.

> from *Gates of Prayer,*
> Reform Judaism Prayerbook

THE JOURNEY

THROUGH

GRIEF

The night I lost you
someone pointed me towards
the Five Stages of Grief.
Go that way, they said,
it's easy, like learning to climb
stairs after the amputation.
And so I climbed.
Denial was first.
I sat down at breakfast
carefully setting the table
for two. I passed you the toast—
you sat there. I passed
you the paper—you hid
behind it.
Anger seemed more familiar.
I burned the toast, snatched
the paper and read the headlines myself.
But they mentioned your departure,
and so I moved on to
Bargaining. What could I exchange
for you? The silence
after storms? My typing fingers?
Before I could decide, *Depression*
came puffing up, a poor relation
its suitcase tied together

with string. In the suitcase
were bandages for the eyes
and bottles of sleep. I slid
all the way down the stairs
feeling nothing.
And all the time Hope
flashed on and off
in defective neon.
Hope was a signpost pointing
straight in the air.
Hope was my uncle's middle name,
he died of it.
After a year I am still climbing,
though my feet slip
on your stone face.
The treeline
has long since disappeared:
green is a color
I have forgotten.
But now I see what I am climbing
towards: *Acceptance*
written in capital letters,
a special headline:
Acceptance,
its name is in lights.
I struggle on,
waving and shouting.
Below, my whole life spreads its surf,
all the landscapes I've ever known
or dreamed of. Below
a fish jumps: the pulse

in your neck.
Acceptance. I finally
reach it.
But something is wrong.
Grief is a circular staircase.
I have lost you.

> Linda Pastan,
> "The Five Stages of Grief"

Three things are fundamental to an understanding of mourning. First, each loss launches us on an inescapable course through grief. Second, each loss revives all past losses. Third, each loss, if fully mourned, can be a vehicle for growth and regeneration.

> Vamik Volkan and
> Elizabeth Zintl,
> *Life After Loss*

Some survivors try to think their way through grief. That doesn't work. Grief is a releasing process, a discovery process, a healing process. . . . The brain must follow the heart at a respectful distance.

> Carol Staudacher,
> *A Time to Grieve*

Charting a Course for Grief

I, who knew very well that the likelihood was that I would be a widow someday, had felt quite sure that if and when it happened I would run to my good friend Helen. In the event, I found that nothing would have dragged me away from the home which was, so to speak, the crown of our thirty years of happy life together. Other widows run away from their home in horror; a few never go back. But our dear house and garden, K's presence there, the friendship of my neighbours, proved the only strength I had. . . .

Grief is an illness of the psyche. To formalize opportunities for its release, for weeping, wailing, yelling at fate is unlikely to help. Tears don't come to order and if they did, how could they bring relief? Rage creeps up on you unawares too. I was coming back from London and as I walked along a crowded compartment and saw people laughing and talking and reading and sleeping something in my mind went briefly out of gear. Their normality was hideous to me. I was in hostile country, an enemy alien.

. . . I had a whole empty house to cry in—but so often the need for tears came when I was at work, when it could not be satisfied. The body's protest at this rigid self-discipline was the quite terrifying exhaustion that came over me at times, so that I could barely lift my hand from the arm of a chair. As with many another woman, the sense of loss sometimes manifested itself in a searing physical pain, somewhere in the guts. It might have gone more easily for me if I had not slammed the door as tightly as I could on recollection of what had happened— I came to think later that I had slammed it against K as well as against anguish—but at the time there was no question of choice. In grief we do as we must . . .

It was a little later that it came to me that there was no one I could talk to. . . . When you are suddenly bereft of your 'speech-friend' (as William Morris called it) you fear that by engaging in conversation with anyone else you are asking a favour. Social assurance is more precarious than we think, for it rests on the assumption that by and large it is mutually agreeable. Gauche adolescents find it impossible to believe that anyone could actually enjoy talking to them; so do people whose inner security has collapsed, through bereavement, divorce, desertion, disgrace, being made redundant or any other reason. I began to have some insight into loneliness . . .

Mary Stott,
Forgetting's No Excuse

LEAN INTO THE PAIN

Grief is a journey. You need to go through it to get through it.

The process is called Grief Work for a very good reason. It *is* work. As painful as it is, it's important to stay on the emotional roller coaster of grief and experience its many feelings. It isn't easy, but the key is to move

toward the pain of grief and feel your feelings in healthy
and healing ways.

> Kathleen Braza,
> on the videotape "To Touch a
> Grieving Heart"

While grief is fresh, every attempt to divert only
  irritates.
You must wait till it be digested. . . .

> Samuel Johnson

GRIEF: THE ONLY WAY OUT IS THROUGH

*You can expect a wide range—even a whirlwind—of feelings
when someone important to you dies or is dying. It may be even
worse if the death was sudden, unexpected, violent, or self-
inflicted, or if it left you with a lot of unfinished business,
emotional and otherwise. Don't feel bad about what you feel; it
is a normal part of grieving. You may not experience all of the
feelings typical of grief, or experience them in a fixed sequence.
But avoiding uncomfortable feelings that do arise will only make
things worse. The work of grieving, and the only way to get
through mourning, is to experience your feelings fully. You may
feel a strong desire to anesthetize your feelings (with food, drugs,
alcohol, sex, work, or busyness) or stuff them. Doing so will only
delay the experience of grief or push it underground; it will
generally express itself anyway, in ways you'll have even less
control over. Don't be surprised if you feel:*

• *Shock, numbness, dazed disbelief, a feeling of just "going through the motions," a sense that part of you is functioning but part of you is not.*

• *Laziness, fatigue, a sense of depletion.*

• *Bewilderment, confusion, indecisiveness, clumsiness, forgetfulness, inability to concentrate, a reduced attention span. Confusion is especially common.*

• *A whirlwind of changing feelings, unexpected surges of emotion, of mental chaos and disintegration, the feeling you might be going mad.*

• *Anger, at the person who died, at the medical establishment, at the people trying to help or console you, at the people who didn't die, at yourself, at whoever gets in the way when the anger feels like coming out; bitterness, hostility.*

• *Pain (both physical and emotional), sorrow, weepiness (tears you have no control over—they won't come when you want them, and then they'll come at times that are embarrassing), despair.*

• *Fear, anxiety, panic, agitation, hypochondria.*

• *A "selfish" preoccupation with your own feelings; a need to be babied, to regress.*

• *Depression, emotional flatness, apathy, defeatism, thoughts of suicide, a feeling of "What's the use?" "Why live?"*

• *Loneliness. A fear of being alone, yet a yearning to be left alone; a need for company, yet no desire to socialize.*

• *A yearning to see and feel the person who died.*

• *The sense of a void, a missing part, an enormous sense of loss and emptiness.*

• *A flood of memories, a restless search for the person who died, a feeling that he or she is nearby or visiting you.*

• *Guilt, regrets ("if only . . ."), ambivalence (especially if you had unfinished business with the person who died), feelings of shame about having "unacceptable" thoughts and emotions.*

• *A mental replaying of the illness, the death, or the life that preceded it; talkativeness, an urge to tell the story of what happened, to talk about the past.*

• *Sleeplessness, overeating or loss of appetite, weight loss or gain, and a wide variety of physical symptoms to which you are unaccustomed.*

• *Conflict with other survivors, or the resurfacing of conflicts from earlier in life—a common problem.*

• *An inability to remember what the dead person looked like; a tendency to idealize (or make a monster of) the dead person; eventually (when you've worked through some grief) the feeling that you are absorbing some of the dead person's personality, that his or her values, qualities, or behaviors are becoming part of you.*

• *Relief that a difficult time has ended.*

• *Acceptance, peace, joy.*

• *Dreams of the deceased; a sense of their presence nearby.*

Pat McNees

STUNNED

I was standing in our dining room, thinking of nothing in particular, when a cablegram was put in my hand. It said, "Susy was peacefully released to-day."

It is one of the mysteries of our nature that a man, all unprepared, can receive a thunderstroke like that and live. There is but one reasonable explanation of it. The intellect is stunned by the shock and but gropingly gathers the meaning of the words. The power to realize their full import is mercifully wanting. The mind has a dim sense of vast loss—that is all. It will take mind and memory months and possibly years to gather the details and thus learn and know the whole extent of the loss. A man's house burns down. The smoking wreckage represents only a ruined home that was dear through years of use and pleasant associations. By and by, as the days and weeks go on, first he misses this, then that, then the other thing. And when he casts about for it he finds that it was in that house. Always it is an *essential*—there was but one of its kind. It cannot be replaced. It was in that house. It is irrevocably lost. He did not realize that it was an essential when he had it; he only discovers it now when he finds himself balked, hampered, by its absence. It will be years before the tale of lost essentials is complete, and not till then can he truly know the magnitude of his disaster.

> Mark Twain (Samuel Clemens),
> whose beloved daughter Susy
> died suddenly of meningitis

SISTER

she was supposed to die slowly
in a starring role
getting more wrinkled moving less fast
turning her head at an angle
as my father does now
to pick up softer parts of conversations
laugh a half second later than others
when the joke made its way to her

she was supposed to take her time
to sit more
and watch more
and be more quiet
to have the luxury
of bitching about her conditions
and laughing with that disgusted smirk
she used so often on democrats
and others with no class or taste

instead:
she went in fast forward
gone at 52
and the speed of it all
is taking us aback

wait a minute:
start the film over
let her have a few more reels

it seems she was
just coming to another subplot

when the credits came on
the lights came up
and we were made to usher ourselves out
the quiet shuffle of feet
betraying our own existence
in our horrid disbelief
that the movie had had its run

John Sherman,
"Finis"

SHOCK AND NUMBNESS—AND GOING THROUGH THE MOTIONS

The Bustle in a House
The Morning after Death
Is solemnest of industries
Enacted upon Earth—

The Sweeping up the Heart
And putting Love away
We shall not want to use again
Until Eternity.

Emily Dickinson

Life must go on,
And the dead be forgotten;
Life must go on,
Though good men die;

Anne, eat your breakfast;
Dan, take your medicine;
Life must go on;
I forget just why.

Edna St. Vincent Millay,
from "Lament"

After great pain, a formal feeling comes—
The Nerves sit ceremonious, like Tombs—
The stiff Heart questions was it He, that bore,
And Yesterday, or Centuries before?

The Feet, mechanical, go round—
Of Ground, or Air, or Ought—
A Wooden way
Regardless grown,
A Quartz contentment, like a stone—

This is the Hour of Lead—
Remembered, if outlived,
As Freezing persons, recollect the Snow—
First—Chill—then Stupor—then the letting go—

Emily Dickinson

DENIAL

The distance that the dead
have gone
Does not at first appear

Their coming back seems
possible
For many an ardent year.

Emily Dickinson

Seeing things as they really are is very painful when a child dies. Ruthless fact is the last thing we want. Somewhere in the back of our minds, especially at first, is the idea that this is all a dream. He couldn't really be dead. She just could not be gone. We will wake up and it will only have been a dream. . . .

Ultimately, though, facing that reality is what we need in order to go on with life when a child is dead. Facing it could well begin with something as simple as language. Robby did not "pass on." Nor did he "fly to heaven" or "go to his just reward."

He died.

Those two words are cold, brutal, and true.

During the time before I decided to live and not exist, I used such euphemisms in even my innermost thoughts. It was only when I could think "Robby is dead" that I could also think "but I am alive."

Harriet Sarnoff Schiff,
The Bereaved Parent

ANGER

American men tend to express grief through anger or through action rather than through tears, says grief therapist Tom Golden, whereas women tend to express even their anger through tears. The anger of grief may be directed toward God, toward the person who died, or anywhere in between. Golden tells the story of one woman who was beautifully in touch with her anger. Every time the grief therapist came to visit her, he found her driving up and down the driveway. One day he asked what she was doing and she explained that every day she would come home, get her recently deceased husband's ashes out of the urn in the living room, take a small amount of ashes and place them on the driveway. "It helps me to run over the son of a bitch every day," she said. This woman's ritual was "good grief," said the therapist, because it was her way of connecting with and expressing the anger component of her grief. Too often people stifle anger because it is not rational, but emotions are not rational. You can love someone and still feel angry that they left you. Grief counselors say that it is important to try to find healing ways to express the anger of grief.

    Sometimes we are angry at those who try to console us.

Immortal? I feel it and know it,
Who doubts it of such as she?
But that is the pang's very secret,—
Immortal away from me.

There's a narrow ridge in the graveyard
Would scarce stay a child in his race,

But to me and my thought it is wider
Than the star-sown vague of Space.

Your logic, my friend, is perfect,
Your moral most drearily true;
But, since the earth clashed on her coffin,
I keep hearing that, and not you.

Console if you will. I can bear it;
'Tis a well-meant alms of breath;
But not all the preaching since Adam
Has made Death other than Death.

It is pagan; but wait till you feel it, —
That jar of our earth, that dull shock
When the ploughshare of deeper passion
Tears down to our primitive rock.

Communion in spirit! Forgive me,
But I, who am earthly and weak,
Would give all my incomes from dreamland
For a touch of her hand on my cheek . . .

James Russell Lowell,
from "After the Burial"

And sometimes we are angry at death itself.

I am not resigned to the shutting away of loving hearts
  in the hard ground.
So it is, and so it will be, for so it has been time out
  of mind:
Into the darkness they go, the wise and the lovely.
  Crowned
With lilies and with laurel they go; but I am not
  resigned.

Lovers and thinkers, into the earth with you,
Be one with the dull, the indiscriminate dust.
A fragment of what you felt, of what you knew,
A formula, a phrase remains—but the best is lost.

The answers quick and keen, the honest look, the
  laughter, the love—
They are gone. They are gone to feed the roses.
  Elegant and curled
Is the blossom. Fragrant is the blossom. I know. But I
  do not approve.
More precious was the light in your eyes than all the
  roses of the world.

Down, down, down into the darkness of the grave
Gently they go, the beautiful, the tender, the kind;
Quietly they go, the intelligent, the witty, the brave.
I know. But I do not approve. And I am not resigned.

> Edna St. Vincent Millay,
> "Dirge Without Music"
> (Millay survived her husband of
> twenty-six years, then died the
> next year herself.)

"The doctors said she would go out like a candle: it wasn't like that, it wasn't like that at all," said my sister, sobbing.

"But, Madame," replied the nurse, "I assure you it was a very easy death."

. . . There is no such thing as a natural death: nothing that happens to a man is ever natural, since his presence calls the world into question. All men must die: but for every man his death is an accident and, even if he knows it and consents to it, an unjustifiable violation.

Simone de Beauvoir,
A Very Easy Death

SORROW AND PAIN

Give sorrow words; the grief that does not speak
Whispers the o'er fraught heart and bids it break.

William Shakespeare

Where there is sorrow, there is holy ground.

Oscar Wilde,
De Profundis

Some heard or saw nothing, but felt again that pang, nameless and centered below the throat, of sorrow which had become . . . like an organ in their flesh.

> Louise Bogan,
> quoted by Carol Staudacher
> in *A Time to Grieve*

Stop all the clocks, cut off the telephone,
Prevent the dog from barking with a juicy bone,
Silence the pianos and with muffled drum
Bring out the coffin, let the mourners come.

Let aeroplanes circle moaning overhead
Scribbling on the sky the message He Is Dead,
Put crêpe bows round the white necks of the public
   doves,
Let the traffic policemen wear black cotton gloves.

He was my North, my South, my East and West,
My working week and my Sunday rest,
My noon, my midnight, my talk, my song;
I thought that love would last for ever: I was wrong.

The stars are not wanted now: put out every one;
Pack up the moon and dismantle the sun;
Pour away the ocean and sweep up the wood;
For nothing now can ever come to any good.

> W. H. Auden,
> "Stop All the Clocks"

I walked a mile with Pleasure,
  And ne'er a word said she;
But oh, the things I learned from her
  When Sorrow walked with me!

Robert Browning Hamilton

Truly, it is allowed to weep. By weeping, we disperse
  our wrath;
and tears go through the heart, even like a stream.

Ovid

There is no wisdom in useless and hopeless sorrow, but
there is something in it so like virtue that he who is
wholly without it cannot be loved.

Samuel Johnson

My life closed twice before its close;
It yet remains to see
If Immortality unveil
A third event to me,

So huge, so hopeless to conceive,
As these that twice befell.
Parting is all we know of heaven,
And all we need of hell.

Emily Dickinson

LOSS

I used to wonder that other men and women were alive when death had come to my friend, whom I had loved as though he would never die. Even more I wondered that I, who was his other self, was still alive when he was dead. Someone once spoke of his friend as "the half of my own soul." I agree, for I felt that my soul and that of my friend had been one soul in two bodies. So I had a horror of going on living, because I did not wish to live on as a half-person. And perhaps, too, that was the reason why I was afraid to die—lest he, whom I had loved so much, should die completely.

Saint Augustine of Hippo,
The Confessions

That the world will never be quite—what a cliché—
   the same again
Is what we only learn by the event
When a friend dies out on us and is not there
To share the periphery of a remembered scent

Or leave his thumb-print on a shared ideal;
Yet it is not at floodlit moments we miss him most
. . . it is in killing
Time where he could have livened it, such as the drop-
   by-drop
Of games like darts or chess . . .

Louis MacNeice,
abridged from "Tam Cari Capitis"

THE NEED TO TALK,
TO REMINISCE

Friends of Jacqueline Kennedy were shocked when, almost immediately after the President's assassination, she compulsively asked people, "Do you want to hear about it?" and rattled off each frame of that terrible sequence in her soft, shaken voice. But their shock reflected their ignorance. Mrs. Kennedy was instinctively helping herself to face the reality. Verbal repetition eventually dulls the horrendous shock enough so that it can be faced, can be accepted.

Talking helps us absorb less tragic situations, but even then, listeners tend to resist. . . . Why? Because it makes them feel uncomfortable. Vulnerable. Such intimations of mortality are frightening to most of us. Our fear outweighs our desire to help.

So from within and without, there are pressures on the widow not to talk. It takes strength to disregard them. Some women have such emotional sturdiness that they immediately set about the work of defining their loss and repeating its circumstances until the cruel edge is blunted enough for them to handle its reality. Other women require months before they can bring themselves to talk about their husbands, about their deaths. And until they can talk, they have not really started on the road to recovery.

Lynn Caine,
Widow

SEARCHING

The bereaved have lost someone infinitely significant for whom there is no substitute. They have this urgent restless need to search and to find; their searching is natural in their loss, but it cannot succeed because the object they seek is a living person. The one they so desperately need to find, for whom they must search and search, is the one they know and love. They seek the living: their search is vain because the one they love is no longer alive. . . .

To find oneself behaving unusually, irrationally, yet restless and frustrated if one tries to stop; not to know why one is doing what it seems one must do; to feel ashamed and foolish and unable to explain; to find no comfort or satisfaction from one's restless activity; this is a bewildering, frightening experience in an already distressing situation. 'Am I going mad?' is the question so often asked, and probably even more often feared and ashamedly unasked.

When something of this concept of loss-and-search is understood, mourners are often relieved and comforted to discover that behaviour which seemed inexplicable, uncontrollable, senseless and disturbing, is a normal universal bereavement experience. This will not ease the urgent need to search, but it goes some way towards relieving the bewilderment and distress. It may make, too, for more compassionate understanding from those around if they are able to recognize something of what lies behind this compulsive restlessness.

Elizabeth Collick,
in *Through Grief,* quoted in
All in the End Is Harvest

We were riding through frozen fields in a wagon at
    dawn.
A red wing rose in the darkness.

And suddenly a hare ran across the road.
One of us pointed to it with his hand.

That was long ago. Today neither of them is alive,
Not the hare, nor the man who made the gesture.

O my love, where are they, where are they going
The flash of a hand, streak of movement, rustle of
    pebbles.
I ask not out of sorrow, but in wonder.

Czeslaw Milosz,
"Encounter"

It happened so often. In her mind she would see a part of him, his hand, his arm, his foot perhaps, in the finely worked leather shoes he always wore, and from it, frantically, she would try to build up the whole man. Sometimes she succeeded better than others, built him up from foot to shoulder, seeing his hands, his grey suit, his tie, knotted always in a slightly special way, his neck, even his chin that was rather sharp, a little less attractive than his other features.

But always at that point she would be defeated. Never once voluntarily since the day he died had she been able to see his face again.

And if she could not remember him, at will, what meaning had time at all? What use was it to have lived the past, if behind us it fell away so sheer?

In the hour of his death, for her it was part of the pain that she knew this would happen. She was standing beside him when, outside the hospital window, a bird called out with a sweet, clear whistle, and hearing it she knew that he was dead, because not for years had she really heard bird-song or bird-call, so loud was the noise of their love in her ears. When she looked down it was a strange face, the look of death itself, that lay on the pillow. And after that brief moment of silence that let in the bird-song for an instant, a new noise started in her head, the noise of a nameless panic that did not always roar, but never altogether died down.

Mary Lavin,
from "In a Cafe"

Depression

I cannot say what loves have come and gone;
I only know that summer sang in me
A little while, that in me sings no more.

> Edna St. Vincent Millay,
> "Sonnets"

There is no greater sorrow than to recall a time of happiness in misery.

> Dante Alighicri

Grief is a very antisocial state.

> Penelope Mortimer

I measure every Grief I meet
With narrow, probing Eyes—
I wonder if it weighs like Mine—
Or has an Easier size.

> Emily Dickinson

I was hollow inside. I was less than half a person. Behind the carefully maintained façade there was nothing, or at least nothing that really mattered. I must try to explain about this phase of bereavement because only those who have been through it know about it, and it is, I am certain, about three months after the death, when many of us appear to be doing quite nicely, that the collapse of the will to live occurs. It is then that widows, and widowers too, especially if they have no dependent children, need to be taken into the care of their friends. What needs to be done is just to keep them ticking over; to ask them on little visits, give them little jobs to do, nothing very much, nothing very demanding, just small things to fill in the emptiness of the personality as well as of the days. At this stage, Death is the friend. Life is the enemy. It seemed to me at this time that being alive was just a habit, and a habit that had now become very disagreeable. Now I had been jolted out of the normal view that it is obviously better to be alive than dead, it seemed a ludicrous proposition. What was so wonderful about being alive? Sixty years of life had habituated me to eating at certain times, washing, dressing, going to work, doing this and that—but *what for?* Why spend another ten or twenty years doing all these things just for the sake of being alive? There were, it is true, fleeting moments of pleasure but there was nothing, *nothing,* that made the future look anything but a dreary, meaningless trudge. The concept of life as a duty, in the abstract, struck me as monstrous. . . .

Mary Stott,
Forgetting's No Excuse

No End to Grief

Did someone say that there would be an end,
An end, Oh, an end, to love and mourning?

May Sarton

Whole years of joy glide unperceived away, while sorrow counts the minutes as they pass.

William Havard

Death may happen in a moment, but grief takes time; and that time is both an ordeal and a blessing. An ordeal in the sense that grief is often one of the most severe mental pains that we must suffer, and a blessing in the sense that we don't have to do it all at once. We can, to a degree, ration out our grief in bearable dosage; according to our circumstances we may choose to give full .vent to grief and, like the Maoris, cry and shout and chant three days and nights on end; or we may stultify our grief, avoiding public show, and leak it, drip by drip, in secret, over many months. But sooner or later, in time, our grief will out, like truth, a harsh reminder of our own mortality.

There are many turning points in the progression of our grief, occasions when events bring home its impact: anniversaries, meetings. . . . At first we think these only serve to aggravate our pain, break down our brittle structures of escape. But, with experience, we learn to treasure them for what they are, reminders of the good things that make up our lives, evidence that "he (or she) lives on in my memory." At last it becomes possible to look back with pleasure and look onward now with hope.

> Colin Murray Parkes,
> in *All in the End Is Harvest*

The worst thing about grief is the length of time during which the experience lasts. For the first weeks one is in a state of shock. But the agony lasts long after the state of shock comes to an end. After a year, or about two, the agony gives way to a dull ache, a sort of void. During the night in one's dreams, and in the morning when one wakes, one is vaguely aware that something is wrong and, when waking is complete, one knows exactly what it is.

> Lord Hailsham of
> St Marylebone,
> in *A Sparrow's Flight*

Ah woe is me! Winter is come and gone,
But grief returns with the revolving year.

> Percy Bysshe Shelley,
> "Adonais"

The face which, duly as the sun,
Rose up for me with life begun,
To mark all bright hours of the day

With homely love, is dimmed away—
And yet my days go on, go on.

The tongue which, like a stream, could run
Smooth music from the roughest stone.
And every morning with "Good day"
Make each day good, is hushed away—
And yet my days go on, go on.

The heart which, like a staff, was one
For mine to lean and rest upon.
The strongest on the longest day
With steadfast love, is caught away—
And yet my days go on, go on . . .

> Elizabeth Barrett Browning,
> "De Profundis"

Grief's Tendency to Isolate

. . . Happiness, of course, is forever bound to place, to the physical world. We are never happy now, only then. Walking then on a Dorset hill, wind lifting the hair, and a hand, suddenly applied at one's back. . . . Happiness is out there, back there, in association with those sights and sounds, and to retrieve it is to retrieve them also, to bring them crowding into the dark bedroom at three in the morning: mocking. Perfect happiness, past perfect, pluperfect.

Unhappiness, now so intimately known, is a very different matter. Unhappiness is now, not then at all. Unhappiness is like being in love: it occupies every moment of every day. It will not be put aside and like love it isolates; grief is never contagious.

Penelope Lively,
in the novel
Perfect Happiness

VISIONS AND VISITATIONS

Why did I dream of you last night?
Now morning is pushing back hair with grey light
Memories strike home, like slaps in the face:
Raised on elbow, I stare at the pale fog
beyond the window.

So many things I had thought forgotten
Return to my mind with stranger pain:
—Like letters that arrive addressed to someone
Who left the house so many years ago.

Philip Larkin

She comes not when Noon is on the roses—
Too bright is Day.
She comes not to the soul till it reposes
From work and play.

But when Night is on the hills, and the great Voices
Roll in from Sea

By starlight and by candlelight and dreamlight
   She comes to me.

                           Herbert Trench

CONFLICT WITH SURVIVORS

Shortly after Robby died, an older couple came to offer condolences. Although they were grandparents, they obviously found it difficult to utter the right words of comfort despite every best intention.

Finally, after an awkward half hour the wife said, "At least you have each other for comfort."

It would seem on the surface that this would be true. After all, both my husband and I had been in the same hospital room, had suffered the same loss, and together had seen our precious child buried.

Certainly having each other for comfort would be the logical solution. Unfortunately, as a number of parents whose child died have discovered, it is impossible to give comfort when you feel an equal grief.

Parents in all walks of life, many now divorced, agreed on the major problem. Too much was expected of the mate and too little was received.

The depth of this phase of the tragedy did not become apparent in the early days after Robby died. My husband and I were too busy trying to put the pieces back together and too busy receiving callers to realize that we could not comfort each other.

Visualize two people pulling a cart for many miles.

When one grows tired, he eases his grip, thereby letting a larger share of the burden fall on the other. The one left pulling grows resentful of the increased burden and voices anger. The first is now resentful because his exhaustion has not been treated sympathetically.

When the positions reverse, the resentment reverses.

Harriet Sarnoff Schiff,
The Bereaved Parent

We were surprised and disappointed that people we thought were good friends became distant, uneasy, and seemed unable to help us. Others who were casual acquaintances became suddenly close, sustainers of life for us. Grief changes the rules, and sometimes rearranges the combinations.

Martha Whitmore Hickman,
in *Healing After Loss*

GUILT, REGRETS, AMBIVALENCE

When death, the great reconciler, has come, it is never our tenderness that we repent of, but our severity.

George Eliot

I remembered, in the bas-relief of shame, the evening I came home from somewhere, to find her leaning on the kitchen sink, washing a stack of dishes I had left undone. "Shut up!" I had shouted when she spoke to me, angered at the robe and slippers, the cane lying on the floor, the medicine bottles, accouterments of a mother too sick to care for her own. Now we were cut off in mid-sentence. Now I would never be able to tell her how sorry I was for everything.

I still grieve for the words unsaid. Something terrible happens when we stop the mouths of the dying before they are dead. A silence grows up between us then, more profound than the grave. If we force the dying to go speechless, the stone dropped into the well will fall forever before the answering splash is heard.

Faye Moskowitz,
A Leak in the Heart

You, who saw Father only two or three times, have no way of knowing how kind and simple he was. I tried—if not exactly to satisfy him, for I am well aware that I was always the disappointment of his life—at least to show him my affection. At the same time, there were days when I revolted against some of his remarks which seemed to me too sure, too positive, and the other Sunday, I remember, in a political discussion I said some things I shouldn't have. I can't tell you how unhappy I am about it now. It seems as though I had been harsh with someone who even then was no longer able to defend himself. I'd give anything if only I had been all affection and gentleness that evening. But I almost always was. Father's nature was so much nobler than mine. I am always complaining. Father's only thought when he was ill was to keep us from knowing about it. However, these are things I can't yet bear to think about. They cause me so much grief. Life has started again. If only I had an aim, an ambition of any kind, it would help me to bear it. But that isn't the case. My own vague happiness was only the reflection of Father's and Mother's, which I always saw around me, not without remorse, which is even sharper now because I was only its shadow. Now the little incidents in life which made up my happiness are filled with pain. However, it is life starting again, and not just a blunt and brief despair, which could only be temporary. So I shall soon be able to see you again, and I promise no longer selfishly to talk to you about things I can't even explain, because I never spoke of them. I can almost say that I never thought of them. They were my life. But I didn't realize it.

> Marcel Proust,
> from a letter to the
> Comtesse de Noailles, 1903

. . . Here in the Grief Healing Group no one shies away from sobs and misery. Here tears "roll down like mighty waters." When I tell the other members that just the other day someone close to me grew impatient and said, "You can't possibly still be grieving. You and your brother weren't even that close," there is a unanimous nodding of heads. "Nobody wants to be with a sad person," says the attorney. "They grow impatient after two weeks."

My friend was not wrong, my brother and I were not close. The passion of our attachment when he was a young boy turned to later disenchantment. Now that old passion returns and fuels my remorse. I turn the anger, that integral aspect of grief, against myself. Whereas many mourners shake their fists in fury at the space their beloveds have left behind—"How could you go and leave me?"—I am my own accuser. Why had I not been larger-hearted? Why hadn't I included Bobby in my life? Why had there been limits and conditions on my love? I become aware of my most grievous crime: I had been ashamed of him.

Now I am ashamed of myself. Such guilt and ambivalence complicate and extend grief. But how could an outsider understand that no, my brother and I were not close and that is precisely why I grieve. . . .

In the intervening week between meetings, I miss the other members of the group. It's as though fellow sufferers are coated with Krazy Glue, the bonding is so swift and secure. . . .

When I was first married my husband took me to his lifelong summer home and taught me the quirks of wind and sea. . . . When we went to the beach for a swim, he warned, "There's a strong undertow. Should you ever get caught in it, don't fight. Just ride it and eventually you'll be put back on the beach, maybe half a mile away, but there's no danger as long as you don't fight it."

I have often imagined getting caught in that undertow

and I know that even as I heard his words in my ears I would fight rather than float. I am just now learning to float for my life.

> Barbara Lazear Ascher,
> *Landscape Without Gravity*

A Woman Mourned by Daughters

Now, not a tear begun,
we sit here in your kitchen,
spent, you see, already.
You are swollen till you strain
this house and the whole sky.
You, whom we so often
succeeded in ignoring!
You are puffed up in death
like a corpse pulled from the sea;
we groan beneath your weight.
And yet you were a leaf,
a straw blown on the bed,
you had long since become
crisp as a dead insect.
What is it, if not you,
that settles on us now
like satin you pulled down
over our bridal heads?
What rises in our throats
like food you prodded in?
Nothing could be enough.
You breathe upon us now

through solid assertions
of yourself: teaspoons, goblets,
seas of carpet, a forest
of old plants to be watered,
an old man in an adjoining
room to be touched and fed.
And all this universe
dares us to lay a finger
anywhere, save exactly
as you would wish it done.

Adrienne Rich

What we call mourning for our dead is perhaps not so much grief at not being able to call them back as it is grief at not being able to want to do so.

Thomas Mann

CLINGING TO GRIEF

If we identify the grief with the love, we may cling to it to be sure the love lasts, too.

The sorrow for the dead is the only sorrow from which we refuse to be divorced. Every other wound we seek to heal, every other affliction to forget; but this wound we

consider it a duty to keep open; this affliction we cherish
and brood over in solitude.

Washington Irving,
The Sketch-Book

*No grief is greater than that from a child's death. In the
parent's anguish and longing for the child, the grief itself may
become almost a substitute for the child, a tangible connection to
the loss. In Shakespeare's* King John, *Act III, scene 4, King
Philip says to the bereaved Constance, "You are as fond of grief
as of your child," and Constance replies:*

Grief fills the room up of my absent child,
Lies in his bed, walks up and down with me,
Puts on his pretty looks, repeats his words,
Remembers me of all his gracious parts,
Stuffs out his vacant garments with his form;
Then have I reason to be fond of grief.

You can't prevent birds of sorrow flying over your
head—but you can prevent them from building nests in
your hair.

Chinese proverb

Because grief may become a substitute for the dead one, giving up our grief can be the greatest challenge of mourning.

> Mary Jane Moffat,
> in *In the Midst of Winter*

Make bitter weeping, and make passionate wailing, and let thy mourning be according to his desert, and so be comforted for thy sorrow. For of sorrow cometh death, and sorrow of heart will bow down the strength. . . . Give not thy heart unto unending sorrow; put it away, remembering the last end; forget it not, for there is no returning again; him thou shalt not profit, and thou wilt hurt thyself. Remember, for him it was yesterday, and today for thee.

> Ecclesiasticus 38:17

INTERNALIZING THE DEAD
(RECONCILIATION)

This process of internalizing the dead, taking the deceased into oneself and containing him so that he becomes part of one's inner self, is the most important task in mourning. It does not happen immediately: for a varying span of time the bereaved is still in touch with the external presence of the lost person. Once the task of internalizing has been achieved, the dependence on the external presence diminishes and the bereaved becomes able to draw on memories, happy or unhappy, and to share these with others, making it possible to talk, think, or feel about the dead person.

Lily Pincus,
Death and the Family

With you a part of me hath passed away; . . .
But yet I treasure in my memory
Your gift of charity, and young heart's ease,
And the dear honour of your amity;
For these once mine, my heart is rich with these.
And I scarce know which part may greater be—
What I keep of you, or you rob from me.

George Santayana,
from "For These Once Were Mine"

At first, a widow cannot separate her purposes and understanding from the husband who figured so centrally in them: she has to revive the relationship, to continue it by symbols and make-believe, in order to feel alive. But as time goes by, she begins to reformulate life in terms which assimilate the fact of his death. She makes a gradual transition from talking to him "as if he were sitting in the chair beside me," to thinking what he would have said and done, and from there to planning her own and her children's future in terms of what he would have wished until finally the wishes become her own, and she no longer consciously refers them to him. So, too, she recasts her relationship to her children, becoming mother and father to them, incorporating her husband's part in their upbringing as an aspect of herself. In the course of this process she will probably change, in personality, in patterns of behaviour, in what she expects from life. But the change will be gradual enough to sustain a continuity of meaning.

Thus grief is mastered, not by ceasing to care for the dead, but by abstracting what was fundamentally important in the relationship and rehabilitating it. A widow has to give up her husband without giving up all that he meant to her, and this task of extricating the essential meaning of the past and reinterpreting it to fit a very different future, seems to proceed by tentative approximations, momentarily comforting but at first unstable. For a while she may not be able to conceive any meanings in her life except those which are backward-looking and memorial, too tragic to sustain any future. In time, if all goes well, she will begin to formulate a sense of her widowhood which neither rejects nor mummifies the past, but continues the same fundamental purposes.

Until then, she will often be overwhelmed by feelings of disintegration.

Peter Marris,
Loss and Change

People do not die for us immediately, but remain bathed in a sort of *aura* of life which bears no relation to true immortality but through which they continue to occupy our thoughts as when they were alive. It is as though they were traveling abroad.

Marcel Proust,
Remembrance of Things Past

RECOVERY

And time remembered is grief forgotten,
And frosts are slain and flowers begotten,
And in green underwood and cover
　　Blossom by blossom the spring begins.

Algernon Charles Swinburne

Mourning . . . is an undoing. Every minute tie has to be untied and something permanent and valuable recovered and assimilated from the knot. The end is gain, of course. Blessed are they that mourn, for they shall be made strong, in fact. But the process is like all human births, painful and long and dangerous.

Margery Allingham

Though you will have to weep
for when you didn't listen
and didn't want to kiss,
and will suddenly find
much about her precious

and mysterious, I want you to
even more so value yourself,

her pain pulling
the words of balm you do possess,
your energy to clean, fold, feed,
encourage and make arrangements.
Words to remind father and child
the cycle of growth this represents.
And the words for yourself
that will not only help but enhance.

And you will begin again
as you have had to do before
and you will know that change
is the sprouting bulb
in the border of loss.

> Angela Peckenpaugh,
> from "Grief Charm for
> Kathleen"

Your pain is the breaking of the shell
that encloses your understanding.
Even as the stone of the fruit must break,
that its heart may stand in the sun, so must
you know pain.
And could you keep your heart in wonder
at the daily miracles of your life, your pain
would not seem less wondrous than your
joy;

And you would accept the seasons of your
heart, even as you have always accepted
the seasons that pass over your fields.
And you would watch with serenity
through the winters of your grief.
. . . And though in your winter you deny
your spring,
Yet spring, reposing within you, smiles in
her drowsiness and is not offended.

ꜱꜱ

. . . And ever has it been that love knows
not its own depth until the hour of separation.

Kahlil Gibran,
from *The Prophet*

*For many, recovery never comes. They would agree with An-
drea Warren (writing many years after the death of her son):
"We don't recover from grief. If we are lucky and if we are
strong, we simply learn how to live with it."*

THE GROWTH THAT COMES
THROUGH GRIEVING

That which does not kill me makes me stronger.

Friedrich Nietzsche

Grief has a quality of healing in it that is very deep because we are forced to a depth of emotion that is usually below the threshold of our awareness.

Stephen Levine

Grief can be the garden of compassion.

Jelaluddin Rumi

Suffering can be productive. We know that painful experiences of all kinds sometimes stimulate sublimations, or even bring out quite new gifts in some people, who may take to painting, writing or other productive activities under the stress of frustrations and hardships. Others become more productive in a different way—more capable of appreciating people and things, more tolerant in their relationships to others—they become wiser.

Melanie Klein

When you look back at the anguish, suffering, and trau-
mas in our life, you'll see that these are the periods of
biggest growth. After a loss that brings you dreadfully
painful months, you are a different man, a different
woman. Many years later, you will be able to look back
and see the positive things—togetherness in your family,
faith or whatever—that came out of your pain.

Elisabeth Kübler-Ross

If only it were possible for us to see farther than our
knowledge reaches . . . perhaps we would bear our
sadnesses with greater trust than we have in our joys. For
they are the moments when something new has entered
us, something unknown. . . . Perhaps many things inside you have been transformed; perhaps somewhere,
someplace deep inside your being, you have undergone
important changes while you were sad.

Rainer Maria Rilke,
Letters to a Young Poet

A period in the wilderness, if it serves no other purpose,
does at least help one to get one's priorities in order.
The things once assumed to be essential for one's life,
such as the constant company of other people, society's
approval, one's own reputation amongst those who
amount to something in the world's eyes, and the number of important people one knows seem suddenly to
dissolve like a mist of unreality. It is a revelation in those

narrowed circumstances how simple life can be when it is shriven of the accretions of social usage and conformity. What at first seems to be almost too unbearable to confront suddenly widens out into a prospect of inner freedom, perhaps the first opportunity to be oneself since one came to self-awareness when one was a small child. It is at this point that one may begin to know oneself for the first time in one's life. The self one knows is, in fact, a central point within, the secret place which is the cornerstone on which the whole edifice of the person is erected.

Martin Israel,
Living Alone

Should you shield the canyons from the windstorms,
You would never see the beauty of their carvings.

quoted by
Elisabeth Kübler-Ross

In our sleep, Pain that cannot forget
Falls drop by drop upon the Heart
And in our Despair, against our Will
Comes Wisdom through the awful grace of God.

Aeschylus

Finally, the lessons of impermanence taught me this: loss constitutes an odd kind of fullness; despair empties out into an unquenchable appetite for life.

> Gretel Ehrlich,
> in *The Solace of Open Spaces,*
> quoted by Gordon Livingston
> in *Only Spring*

WHEN BAD THINGS HAPPEN TO GOOD PEOPLE

Let me suggest that the bad things that happen to us in our lives do not have a meaning when they happen to us. They do not happen for any good reason which would cause us to accept them willingly. But we can give them a meaning. We can redeem these tragedies from senselessness by imposing meaning on them. The question we should be asking is not, "Why did this happen to me? What did I do to deserve this?" That is really an unanswerable, pointless question. A better question would be "Now that this has happened to me, what am I going to do about it?" . . .

When a person is dying of cancer, I do not hold God responsible for the cancer or for the pain he feels. They have other causes. But I have seen God give such people the strength to take each day as it comes, to be grateful for a day full of sunshine or one in which they are relatively free of pain.

When people who were never particularly strong become strong in the face of adversity, when people who tended to think only of themselves become unselfish and heroic in an emergency, I have to ask myself where they got these qualities which they would freely admit they did not have before. My answer is that this is one of the ways in which God helps us when we suffer beyond the limits of our own strength. . . .

I am a more sensitive person, a more effective pastor, a more sympathetic counselor because of [my son] Aaron's life and death than I would ever have been without it. And I would give up all of those gains in a second if I could have my son back. If I could choose. I would forgo all the spiritual growth and depth which has come my way because of our experiences, and be what I was fifteen years ago, an average rabbi, an indifferent counselor, helping some people and unable to help others, and the father of a bright, happy boy. But I cannot choose.

> Rabbi Harold Kushner,
> *When Bad Things Happen to Good People*

REMEMBRANCE

All that we can know about those we have loved and lost is that they would wish us to remember them with a more intensified realization of their reality. What is es-

sential does not die but clarifies. The highest tribute to
the dead is not grief but gratitude.

Thornton Wilder

It is the great mystery of human life that old grief gradually passes into quiet, tender joy. The mild serenity of
age takes the place of the riotous blood of youth. I bless
the rising sun each day, and, as before, my heart sings to
meet it, but now I love even more its setting, its long
slanting rays and the soft, tender, gentle memories that
come with them, the dear images from the whole of my
long, happy life—and over all the Divine Truth, soften-
ing, reconciling, forgiving!

Fyodor Dostoyevsky

We do not remember days, we remember moments.

Cesare Pavese

WORDS FOR ALICE AFTER HER DEATH

It came by surprise
like a blown fuse,
an old car you were used to
for a few errands, stolen.
We made room in our busy lives
to deal with your loss

as we had your illness.
You asked so little
I'm stumped with your elegy.
I'd rather rub your back
at your request,
or deal a hand of gin rummy.
At your own death you might
have let out one of your
high pitched sighs, your
reaction when landing on a chair,
shock of contact,
relief at getting there.

Now your old blue robe,
as familiar as the dark
green kitchen walls
will be in the last load
of laundry. The Fanny Farmer
box that held the savored
chocolate candy will
be emptied in the trash,
another act done
by one or two people
who kept looking in.

There won't be too much to move,
contents of closet, bureau, desk,
a bed and a few old chairs.
We already went through the pantry,
the spare room, eliminating
all but the nostalgic and necessary.

I find myself seeing your smile,
so welcome. It told of pain
for the time forgotten
in the pleasure of my brief company.
You were so grateful
for small acts of kindness
it was easy to feel blessed
for manicure, bed change,
buying a shower cap at the 5 & 10.
I see your white hair, eyes peeking
over the front door glass,
a blown kiss to assure me
you were safe inside,
but, frail package, how could
you be, really. That was
the old nurse's trick, to grin
and bear it, inquire about my health
first thing by phone call
in the morning. Yes,
you remembered my latest worry
and gave it an airing, before
we decided when I would see you.
I forgive you your resistances
to my consoling schemes—
for turning down good mystery books
because your eyes were failing,
for wearing the dress from India
only once, because the sleeves were tight,
and for picking at a Chinese dish
in a restaurant I had chosen.

Now I regret how little
your coin collection added up to
when I took it to the gold exchange.
The clerk said sometimes customers
salted the kitty for grandmothers
because they couldn't believe
how little their life savings
had come to. How little it all
comes to. But I used to remind you
at least you had interesting friends—
Buddhists and poets, an actor or two
and you agreed. And left alone
stains of fear and disease
on the sheets but didn't stain
our consciences with demands
we couldn't answer.
"What is the name of those beans?"
you wanted to know, embarrassed
to have forgotten.
I think I said every kind—pinto, string,
lima, green. But it was an avocado
that Jeff brought you,
on your mind. Hard to grasp,
like your bravery at the end,
trips down the old steps
to the washing machine,
outings in the car
to our affairs, picnic, rummage sale,
art show, when for you
a slow walk from bed to front room
must have seemed a trip to the moon.

It was no small feat
to heat up hamburger and add frozen
potatoes to the grease,
creating a little Yorkshire pudding,
that left you pleased.
Your presence now is like the backrub
you tried to give me—the touch is
weak but gentle, and full of apology.

                    Angela Peckenpaugh

In the beginning, memory is a nightstalker and imagination its cruel accomplice. Why, why? What if, what if?

Lying tangled and sweating in a nightmare of lost possibilities, we await the mercy of morning.

The dawn brings an unlikely companion: the past has become a friend. This is the surprise we have been waiting for. Suddenly, there is no struggle to hide from memory and imagination. Suddenly, memory is sweet and imagination liberating.

                    Molly Fumia,
                    in *Safe Passage: Words to Help the
                    Grieving Hold Fast and Let Go*

OLD HABITS DIE HARD: MILK

the way I keep shaking the milk
long after the cream is mixed by machine
long after I started drinking milk

without cream. Pale drops splatter
when the seal is broken.

the way the cat keeps leaping on the screen
clinging white belly and eyes
long after my neighbor said
stop feeding it.

the way I keep reaching for the phone
to lap up your voice
long after you've gone
long after you've gone

Patti Tana

Nothing Can Bring
Back the Hour

There was a time when meadow, grove, and stream,
The earth, and every common sight,
   To me did seem
  Apparelled in celestial light,
The glory and the freshness of a dream.
It is not now as it hath been of yore;—
  Turn wheresoe'er I may,
    By night or day,
The things which I have seen I now can see no more.

   The Rainbow comes and goes,
   And lovely is the Rose,
   The Moon doth with delight
Look round her when the heavens are bare;

Waters on a starry night
Are beautiful and fair;
The sunshine is a glorious birth;
But yet I know, where'er I go,
That there hath past away a glory from the earth.

Our birth is but a sleep and a forgetting:
The Soul that rises with us, our life's Star,
  Hath had elsewhere its setting,
    And cometh from afar:
  Not in entire forgetfulness,
  And not in utter nakedness,
But trailing clouds of glory do we come
    From God, who is our home:
Heaven lies about us in our infancy! . . .

  Though nothing can bring back the hour
Of splendour in the grass, of glory in the flower;
  We will grieve not, rather find
  Strength in what remains behind;
  In the primal sympathy
  Which having been must ever be;
  In the soothing thoughts that spring
  Out of human suffering;
  In the faith that looks through death,
In years that bring the philosophic mind.

William Wordsworth,
from "Ode: Intimations of
Immortality"

Unresolved Losses
and Unfinished Business

Grief is the emotion that accompanies mourning and we grieve on a recurring basis as we face the commonplace losses that line our lives—be it the loss of an heirloom earring, a hope, an ideal, a friendship, a homeland, a loved one, or even a former self. . . . The course of our lives depends on our ability to make these breaks, to adapt to all losses, and to use change as a vehicle for growth. Losses not fully mourned—in other words, changes to which we cannot adapt—shadow our lives, sap our energy and impair our ability to connect. If we are unable to mourn, we stay in the thrall of old issues, dreams, and relationships, out of step with the present because we are still dancing to tunes from the past. . . . unresolved losses color our lives, permeating our ability to negotiate even such routine exchanges as greetings, leavetakings, and appointment-making. . . .

> Vamik Volkan and
> Elizabeth Zintl,
> *Life After Loss*

Unfinished business from the past doesn't simply disappear. If it is not dealt with, it remains buried inside. Then, the wounded inner child resurfaces later in unexpected and troubling ways.

> Stephanie Covington and
> Liana Beckett

Thus depression, when it finally came to me, was in fact no stranger, not even a visitor totally unannounced; it had been tapping at my door for decades.

. . . The genetic roots of depression seem now to be beyond controversy. But I'm persuaded that an even more significant factor was the death of my mother when I was thirteen; this disorder and early sorrow—the death or disappearance of a parent, especially a mother, before or during puberty—appears repeatedly in the literature on depression as a trauma sometimes likely to create nearly irreparable emotional havoc. The danger is especially apparent if the young person is affected by what has been termed "incomplete mourning"—has, in effect, been unable to achieve the catharsis of grief, and so carries within himself through later years an insufferable burden of which rage and guilt, and not only dammed-up sorrow, are a part, and become the potential seeds of self-destruction.

William Styron,
Darkness Visible: A Memoir of Madness

HELPING
THE BEREAVED

Once I made people tell me their labour stories. Now I want to hear their death stories—the heart attacks, the car crashes, the cancers, the morgues. I start to believe that there's such a thing as a "good" or "easy" death, just as there is a "good" or "easy" birth. And I start to write to friends when their fathers die, something I never used to do, something I feel ashamed at not having done before.

> Blake Morrison,
> *And When Did You Last See Your*
> *Father?*

The dancer Isadora Duncan lost both her children when a taxi they were riding in became submerged in water. She speaks here of the Italian actress Eleanora Duse.

[Eleanora Duse] used to rock me in her arms, consoling my pain, but not only consoling, for she seemed to take my sorrow to her own breast, and I realised that if I had not been able to bear the society of other people, it was because they all played the comedy of trying to cheer me with forgetfulness. Whereas Eleanora said:

"Tell me about Deirdre and Patrick," and made me

repeat to her all their little sayings and ways, and show her their photos, which she kissed and cried over. She never said, "Cease to grieve," but she grieved with me, and, for the first time since their death, I felt I was not alone.

Isadora Duncan,
My Life

But in those early days, I discovered a marvelously soothing balm, the condolence letter. I had never before understood its function. If I thought of it at all, it was simply a duty like a bread-and-butter letter. But to the widow, a letter gives comfort without demanding the intimacy that she cannot give or, at least, that I could not give. I was grateful for the thought, the comfort, the remembrance. I was also grateful that I did not have to react instantly to show my gratitude. Letters were a source of strength, of comfort.

Lynn Caine,
Widow

At the newspaper where I work, I note that I am dividing people into two camps, those who offer their condolences and those who do not. My friend Betsy has warned me that this will happen, that she went through the same thing when her father died, but I did not think then that I would do this now.

To those who say they are sorry, I gratefully say thank you, so am I. For those who studiously avoid me, avoid looking me straight on, avoid saying a single word, I have nothing but contempt. I know that I am being small and meanspirited. I know that for many people it is difficult to approach a person locked in grief, but I know, too, that at this point in what is left of my life I am not the most forgiving person I know.

> Ruth Coughlin,
> *Grieving: A Love Story*

We have much more to offer than we may realize. All we have to do is ask "How can I help?" with an open heart, and then really listen.

> Ram Dass and Paul Gorman,
> *How Can I Help?*

If honest emotion is shared, the response tends to be compassionate, but if those who grieve don't bring up the subject of fatal illness and death, no one else will. Those who would comfort us are watching our eyes, awaiting our lead. No one can know how to help unless we teach them. Everyone is so unnerved by death that they feel inadequate to ease the pain of those it has robbed. Perhaps that explains letters, which at the time of Bobby's death failed to comfort, those that said, "Call if you need anything." "Let us know what we can do."

Now I understand that the correspondents were frightened and needed us to show them what to do, how to act. Needed us to let them know that they were safe, that our pain could not magically become theirs should we touch. That bad luck is not contagious. They could not know that no one in mourning will respond to cautious invitation. Mourners need the brave souls who dare to hold them, touch them, to stay rather than leave when the tears begin to flow. They do not need sage advice or perfect words. Simple human touch is the mourner's balm.

Perhaps that is why the Grief Healing Group was an important companion on my journey through sorrow. It provided a safe place to cry, an atmosphere of quiet empathy. We expected nothing of ourselves, neither to comfort nor be comforted, we were merely there with our grief. And we were not alone.

Barbara Lazear Ascher,
Landscape Without Gravity

In interviewing people who have facilitated such groups, one common grievance expressed by most participants is the silence of their friends. Among friends, there is a lack of candor or even willingness to mention, let alone talk about, death. People who mourn are often (though certainly not always) ready to talk, to share memories and reflections on the meaning of life and the importance this person had on the lives of the people who are still alive. Talk about the deceased. You will find out quickly whether it is appreciated. Do not assume that a friend wants to mourn alone. Few mourners want privacy for very long. Most want and need contact.

Sol Gordon,
Is There Anything I Can Do?

Mourning the Death of a Child

My Child Is Dead

My child is dead, and I am dying. I am killed by grief, crushed by the enormity of being alive, consumed by self-hate because it was my job as his parent to protect him and I could not. For that I do not deserve to live.

They say the bereaved experience stages—denial, then anger, depression, blame, and finally acceptance. But grief is not clear cut for me. It swoops and swirls and cuts me off and knocks me down, running helter-skelter from stage to stage and back again while I yearn for my own death because maybe, maybe, oh *please* maybe, I would be reunited with my little boy.

Still, I cannot let go of life. I understand so little of this process of grief, yet this I know for sure: The theory about stages is wrong. We bereaved don't reach acceptance. We don't recover from grief. If we are lucky and if we are strong, we simply learn how to live with it.

We live to honor the memories of our loved ones. They deserve no less from us. To make our lives count is our penance for living.

> Andrea Warren,
> whose young son was struck by
> a car

Terminal is one of those *nice* terms that doctors use instead of the real word. In this instance, the real word is death.

Art Linkletter collected the innocent, witty, and wise sayings of children. Here is one that I collected.

"I heard the doctor tell my mom that I was going to the terminal."

"Do you know what that means?" I asked.

"The terminal is where the trains leave from. I guess I'm going away."

Ted Menten,
Gentle Closings

SARAH, AGE SEVEN

In the days shortly before her death, she would lie curled up in a chair, half-dozing, half-watching us as we lived out our lives around her. Smiling, she would say, "I'm so happy, I feel I've got arms tight round me." Her death was the most exciting moment of my life. Deep in the almost overwhelming pain and grief of her going I was still conscious of a great joy and triumph; joy that she had not been destroyed by her suffering, that she was still confident and reassured; joy that we were able to hand her back into and on to the greatest Love of all; joy that this was not really the end. I felt a very real sense of a new birth—more painful but as exciting as her first one seven years earlier. There was an inexplicable but un-shakable knowledge that all was indeed well.

> Jane Davies,
> from *The Price of Loving,*
> reprinted in *All in the End Is Harvest*

There is something disorderly about the death of a young person. In a universe disturbed by so much over which we have no control, an untimely tragedy rattles the teeth of our already shaken confidence. We want to domesticate death, fight it on our own turf, in familiar rooms with shades drawn evenly, top sheets turned back, and a circle of hushed voices closing in.

> Faye Moskowitz,
> *A Leak in the Heart*

Dealing with a loss like the death of a child is more like learning how to live after a part of you has been cut off than it is like healing from a wound.

> Tom Golden,
> *A Man's Grief*

Although we know that after such a loss the acute state of mourning will subside, we also know we shall remain inconsolable and will never find a substitute. No matter what may fill the gap, even if it be filled completely, it nevertheless remains something else.

> Sigmund Freud, on the early
> loss of his daughter

I Wish We Had Loved Johnny More When He Was Alive

My grief, I find, is not desolation or rebellion at universal law or deity. I find grief to be much simpler and sadder. Contemplating the Eternal Deity and His Universal Laws leaves me grave but dry-eyed. But a sunny fast wind along the Sound, good sailing weather, a new light boat, will shame me to tears: how Johnny would have loved this boat, this wind, this sunny day! . . .

Missing him now, I am haunted by my own shortcomings, how often I failed him. I think every parent must have a sense of failure, even of sin, merely in remaining alive after the death of a child. One feels that it is not right to live when one's child has died, that one should somehow have found the way to give one's life to save his life. Failing there, one's failures during his too brief life seem all the harder to bear and forgive. How often I wish I had not sent him away to school when he was still so young that he wanted to remain at home in his own room, with his own things and his own parents. How I wish we had maintained the marriage that created the home he loved so much. How I wish we had been able before he died to fulfill his last heart's desires: the talk with Professor Einstein, the visit to Harvard Yard, the dance with his friend Mary.

These desires seem so simple. How wonderful they would have been to him. All the wonderful things in life are so simple that one is not aware of their wonder until they are beyond touch. Never have I felt the wonder and beauty and joy of life so keenly as now in my grief that Johnny is not here to enjoy them.

Today, when I see parents impatient or tired or bored with their children, I wish I could say to them, But they are alive, think of the wonder of that! They may be a care and a burden, but think, they are alive! You can touch them—what a miracle! You don't have to hold back sudden tears when you see just a headline about the Yale-Harvard game because you know your boy will never see the Yale-Harvard game, never see the house in Paris he was born in, never bring home his girl, and you will not hand down your jewels to his bride and will have no grandchildren to play with and spoil. Your sons and daughters are alive. Think of that—not dead but alive! Exult and sing.

All parents who have lost a child will feel what I mean. Others, luckily, cannot. But I hope they will embrace them with a little added rapture and a keener awareness of joy.

I wish we had loved Johnny more when he was alive. Of course we loved Johnny very much. Johnny knew that. Everybody knew it. Loving Johnny more. What does it mean? What can it mean, now?

Parents all over the earth who lost sons in the war have felt this kind of question, and sought an answer. To me, it means loving life more, being more aware of life, of one's fellow human beings, of the earth.

It means obliterating, in a curious but real way, the ideas of evil and hate and the enemy, and transmuting them, with the alchemy of suffering, into ideas of clarity and charity.

It means caring more and more about other people, at home and abroad, all over the earth. It means caring more about God.

I hope we can love Johnny more and more till we too die, and leave behind us, as he did, the love of love, the love of life.

> Frances Gunther,
> in *Death Be Not Proud* by John
> Gunther, an account of their
> son's death from a brain tumor

What Really Matters

When we went back to Washington at the end of the summer, we became aware of a change in ourselves. We were thinking far more than ever before about what really matters in life, about feelings, about the more abiding human values, about people—people as individuals. Jane talked of all these matters in her last weeks, and she made them more real to us than they had been. She also took pleasure in passing on her more cherished possessions to her friends. She gave a lot of thought to it. She liked to see them walk away with something she had given them, after they had said good-bye.

"I don't need a 'thing' to remember Jane by," said one of her friends. "Jane taught me how to make bread. Whenever I make bread, I think of her."

Before she died, we had talked of how people live on in what they do, in their actions, in the memories of those they have influenced. That was how Jane hoped she would live on. And she will.

> Rosemary and Victor Zorza,
> *A Way to Die,* about the death
> of their daughter Jane at
> twenty-five

FOR A CHILD BORN DEAD

What ceremony can we fit
You into now? If you had come
Out of a warm and noisy room
To this, there'd be an opposite
For us to know you by. . . .
But we have never seen you stride
Ambitiously the world we know.
You could not come and yet you go. . . .
Then all our consolation is
That grief can be as pure as this.

> Elizabeth Jennings
> (abridged)

You Never Thought . . .

You probably never thought you could live through your child's funeral. What could have been more dreadful? But you did.

Certainly surviving all the grief you felt seemed impossible. Those days and nights of crying, exhaustion, and pain were almost beyond endurance. You were certain, at times, you would never get past that time in your life. But you did.

There were times you felt great guilt because somehow you had not filled the role of 'parent' as society interprets the role. You were unable to save your child and keep it alive. As that cold, clammy feeling would come over you and your back would prickle thinking about what you could have done differently, you were sunk into such a pit of grieving that you never dreamed it would be possible to go on. But you did.

Often, you were beset with anger and a feeling of powerlessness because events that should have been in your control simply were not. You did not think you could overcome these feelings—especially the hopelessness that accompanied them. But you can.

Just when you needed your mate most, you would find he or she could help you least. You expected comfort from someone incapable of comforting. You argued. Sometimes you even hated. You never thought you would rise from the bottom of the well of sorrow. But you can.

You thought never again could you take an interest in the world and retain friendships and attend weddings and happy occasions for other people's children. You were certain you could never live through the trauma. But you will.

There was no doubt in your mind that you never again could enjoy yourself. Never want to travel. Never give parties—or attend them. Never have fun. You would only be sorrowful and certainly you would never laugh. Above all, not laugh. But you will.

And most of all, you were sure it would be impossible for you to function as a whole human being not buffeted by the waves of sorrow that swept over you in the early days of your tragedy. But you will.

You will do all that and you will do more.

> Harriet Sarnoff Schiff,
> *The Bereaved Parent*

Mourning the Death of a Parent

Our parents . . . provide a barrier against death, and when both of them are gone . . . there is nothing between us and our own mortality.

Elizabeth Forsythe Hailey,
A Woman of Independent Means

When My Father Died

I didn't realize that it would be such a physical thing. A death—especially the sudden death of a loved one—is a violent act on your body. I felt very much as if I'd been hit by a plank around the shoulders and the chest. My head felt heavy. It was a stunning experience. . . . I felt like someone stole him from me in the middle of the night. . . . There's such a compelling wish in all of us to be reunited with the people we love. It's so unfathomable when people you love aren't here anymore.

Marlo Thomas,
about the death of her father,
Danny Thomas

When did you last see your father? Was it when they burnt the coffin? Put the lid on it? When he exhaled his last breath? When he last sat up and said something? When he last recognized me? When he last smiled? When he last did something for himself unaided? When he last felt healthy? When he last thought he might be healthy, before they brought the news? The weeks before he left us, or life left him, were a series of depletions; each day we thought "he can't get less like himself than this," and each day he did. I keep trying to find the last moment when he was still unmistakably there, in the fullness of his being, *him.*

My father wouldn't approve of morbidity. When I hear his voice in my head appraising what I'm writing about him, he doesn't approve of that either: "You fathead. Seventy-five bloody years, over forty of them while you were alive yourself, and all we get is me looking like death warmed up. You daft sod—do you think that dying is anything to write home about, that it's any sort of story? Let's hear about some of the good times, the holidays, the golf and tennis. What's the big deal about death? No, tell them how good with my hands I could be, all the fun we had and things we built, how I loved you and Gill and Mummy, how I tried to leave the world a better place."

Blake Morrison,
*And When Did You Last See Your
Father?*

WHEN MY MOTHER DIED

There was a "Peanuts" cartoon [in which] Charlie Brown talks about being in the back seat of a car with his mom and dad driving home. That cartoon conjured up safe thoughts and comforting images for me. The cartóon ends with Charlie Brown pointing out that, of course, this doesn't last, that you grow up and never get to sleep in the back seat again. That is how I felt when my mom died; I could never again sleep in the back seat. I had to be in the driver's seat.

> Karen Kandik,
> in "Finding Home"

A LICK AND A PROMISE

How can I remember the Christmases of my childhood, the good, the less good, without remembering bringing Joan from the nursing home for Christmas celebrations—and bringing her back afterwards? I feel best about her first Christmas away from the nursing home, when we took her to a friend's home with a big tree, and she looked at it with eyes wide like a child's and said, "It's beautiful!" When we brought out the presents, she was astonished at how many were for her. "All of these are for me?" I felt at that moment as if she were my daughter, as well as my mother.

Her condition would last for a while on a sort of plateau and then drop to a worse state. The pattern was repeated again and again.

After about six years, she became so dim that visits hardly seemed to bring her a moment of happiness. She didn't look at the flowers I brought or eat the cookies. She didn't register any pleasure at my presence. Nothing seemed to help. On the advice of friends, I drastically cut back on the visits. They made me hysterical—I would hyperventilate as soon as I left the floor where her room was—and didn't appear to help her. I don't know whether I did the right thing. I fear that during the years when I didn't visit much she had clearer spells that I missed.

She died the night before her seventy-eighth birthday. I thought, "What a good present for her." At last I knew that she was neither lonely, frightened, in pain nor abysmally bored.

I have always dreamed about her, but for many years dreamed only of the Alzheimer's disease Joan, not of my mother before the Alzheimer's. Now, I dream of her as her old self, always feel that each dream is a gift from her, almost like a visit.

I want her. How is it possible not to want your mother? How is it possible not to miss her love?

I find myself using expressions that she used, like, "Too much of a muchness," "That gives me the heebie-jeebies," or "I'll give it a lick and a promise" (I'll clean it just a bit.). They pop into my head. I'm making a list of them.

Carol Anne Douglas,
in "My Mother, My Joan"

You thought it heartless
When my father fell down
Dead in his splendid prime,
Strong as a green oak thrown,
That all I did was praise
Death for this kindness,
Sang with a voice unbroken
Of the dear scholar's days,
His passion of a lifetime—
And my loss never spoken.

Judge of another's grief?
Weigh out that grief in tears?
I did not weep my father,
The rich, the fulfilled years.
What slow death have you known?
When no hope or belief
Can help, no loving care?
We watch and weep alone.
My heart broke for my mother.
I buried grief with her.

It is the incomplete,
The unfulfilled, the torn
That haunts our nights and days
And keeps us hunger-born.
Grief spills from our eyes,
Unwelcome, indiscreet,
As if sprung from a fault
As rivers seam a rock
And break through under shock.
We are shaken by guilt.

There are some griefs so loud
They could bring down the sky,
And there are griefs so still
None knows how deep they lie,
Endured, never expended.
There are old griefs so proud
They never speak a word;
They never can be mended.
And these nourish the will
And keep it iron-hard.

May Sarton,
"Of Grief"

A CHILD'S GRIEF

When my father was an old man, he surprised me by remarking that he understood what my mother's death meant to me but had no idea what to do about it. I think it would have been something if he had just said this.

William Maxwell,
So Long, See You Tomorrow

Children's griefs are little, certainly: but so is the child, so is its endurance, so is its field of vision, while its nervous impressionability is keener than ours. Grief is a matter of relativity; the sorrow should be estimated by its proportion to the sorrower: a gash is as painful to one as an amputation to another.

Francis Thompson

Forced to create my own rituals for grief, I begin a secret, fictional diary about a little girl and her mother. Setting it in 1933, I "illustrate" the diary with pictures from my stepmother's magazines that look old-fashioned to me. One that makes a particularly strong impression on me features a mother and daughter in a sunny kitchen dominated by an old wood range. I glue the picture into my diary and write underneath it, "After school today, Mommy and I made cookies together." Each week I fold my entries carefully in an empty cottage cheese container and bury it in the garden. I call the containers "time capsules" and believe that someone will find them someday and learn the truth. It doesn't occur to me until years later that in the act of creating the "diary," I was burying the dead in the only way I knew how to. Those scraps of folded paper and magazine pictures I passed off as my own were like seeds that I planted, opening later into the story that is my life as it has bloomed even without her. . . .

I am forever different from my women friends who still have their mothers. I am not the same woman I would have been if she'd lived. And I did not, after the age of nine, have the same girlhood. But as to whether either would have been better or worse, I cannot say. All I can say with certainty is that I am haunted by her. That there is a rent, a tear, a rip in the fabric of my life that can't ever be completely sewn up or patched over, but which lets in both the darkness that is the underworld and a world of astonishing—the only word which can describe it is celestial—light. That my mother is both with me and not with me, alive and gone. And, that though these words begin to tell some small part of the story, it is a story I will probably be telling all my life— of a girl and her mother and the love which connects them, like a strong rope, or an umbilical cord, running faithfully between this world and whatever world comes next.

> Alison Townsend,
> from "Small Comforts"
> in *Loss of the Ground-Note*

A FIFTEEN-YEAR-OLD
REMEMBERS HIS MOTHER'S DEATH

I remember the day my mom died very clearly. It was six years ago and I woke up and my dad asked me to go to the library with him because he had to do some research. We said good-bye to Mom and my brother, Tim, who was eleven, and off we went for the rest of the day. When we came back, we saw a big commotion about a block away from our house, and when we got home, Dad called out for Mom, but she wasn't there, so we went to a neighbor's house to see if he knew what was going on, and that's where Timmy was. The neighbor said Mom was at the hospital, and while Dad went there, Timmy told me what had happened. He'd gone out for a walk with Mom and there had been two taxi cabs that crashed into each other. One swiveled around and hit Mom and she hit her head—she was thrown up into the air against a mailbox. I didn't think that the accident was serious—I had this picture of Mom coming home that night with a big bandage around her head, telling some funny story about how it had happened. She would have been so good-humored about the whole thing.

A little later Dad came back to our neighbor's house and took us into the bedroom. He said, "Boys, I have to tell you something. Your mom died." There was a loud wail—really loud and really sudden. I remember hearing Timmy at the same time as myself. We went over and hugged Daddy and we cried for a long time. It was such a shock to me. Then Dad had to make phone calls to Mom's mother and to his parents, and I wanted to be with him while he did this. That night the three of us slept in Dad's room in his bed.

Dad said I didn't have to go to the funeral, but I wanted to. I would feel bad now if I hadn't gone. When I walked in, everyone was looking at me and I felt a strange sort of pride, like "I'm the one you have to feel sorry for." I know it sounds stupid, but that's the way I felt. I felt bad that Mom had died, but I also felt proud that everyone was looking at me, and I wanted to look strong. I didn't cry, because I had done most of my crying. The way I looked at it, there was no need to cry. There was nothing I could do to bring her back. There was no point in living in the past.

I was really mad at Mom. I never blamed the taxi

drivers. I don't know why, but I didn't. I just took it for granted that accidents happen and it wasn't their faults but Mom should have known better. She should have jumped back more quickly like Timmy did. Timmy was mad too—mad that he hadn't been able to pull her back. He felt helpless that he couldn't help her, and that was rough. I even asked Dad, "Do you think Mom knows she's ruined our lives?"

Mom was buried out in Long Island and I've been there only five times. I've never been there on a sunny day, so it's always been dark, and I've always been with someone who's crying. Everything there is ugly. Everything a cemetery represents is terrible—the way they look—orderly and gray, gravestones and slabs. Going there makes me feel worse. It just reminds me that people are going to die, and my worst fear is that *I'm* going to die. That's what I get out of going to a cemetery. When I die, they can bury me at sea or send me into space.

I'd rather remember my mother by thinking about her on her birthday and maybe going to temple on that day. I like it when people tell me stories and I get to know her better. I love finding out more about what she was like, because I was only nine when she died and I didn't know her that well. I mean, I knew her as a mother, not as a person.

Sometimes I see someone from the back who looks like her and I think, "Maybe she's alive and this is all just a cruel joke." I think maybe she's had amnesia and she doesn't know who she is and I'll go tell her.

Last year I read this story that I really related to. It's a horror story called "The Monkey's Paw" where you get three wishes. And this man wishes that his dead son can come back alive. Well, he gets his wish and the son comes back all mutilated because he died in some horrible accident. So the guy reaches for the monkey's paw and wishes him dead again. That's how I feel. I want my mom back, but if she did come back she'd be a vegetable or something. She just wouldn't be Mom.

About a month after she died, I once asked myself if it had to happen over again, would it have been better to have Dad die than to have Mom die. I didn't really answer the question because I felt so guilty about even thinking of it.

The first two years were the hardest. I still get a lump in my throat when I think about Mom, and I still feel bad. It's not as often as it used to be. Dad and I talk about a lot of things, but we don't talk about our feelings as much as we should. On the whole I'm closer to my dad than I ever was, and I know in some ways we couldn't get closer.

The thing about losing a mother is that now I know I can take just about anything. It was so painful, but I survived the loss and it's made me a stronger person.

Last year Dad got remarried to Karen and we're more of a family now. It's still a little weird to have people call up and ask for Mrs. Davis and it's not Mom. The first time it happened, someone called and said, "Hello, is Mrs. Davis there?" I never said, "Wait a minute." I said, "No, she's dead."

For a while I didn't think Karen had any right to tell me motherly things like "Wash your hands," "Eat your vegetables,'' or "Clean your room"—things like that. In fact, I still don't like it. I know she has the right to discipline me, but I prefer it when my father tells me what to do. And he's still the one I always ask if I want permission to go somewhere.

Jesse was born three months ago and he's a very unifying element. We can all relate to the baby. In some ways I'm his brother, but in other ways I'm just his half-brother. I'm his brother because we do things together and I take care of him. I'm his half-brother because I call Karen "Karen" and he's going to call her "Mom." I could never call Karen "Mom" and I sort of wish he couldn't either so that we could be perfect brothers. I wish that his mom was my mom and he would feel what I feel about Mom. As it is, he'll never know.

> Nick Davis, age fifteen,
> one of eighteen children telling
> stories in Jill Krementz's book,
> *How It Feels When a Parent Dies*

Death ends a life but it does not end the relationship, which struggles in the survivor's mind towards some final resolution, some clear meaning, which it perhaps never finds.

> Robert W. Anderson,
> from the play *I Never Sang for
> My Father*

A WOMAN MOURNS THE DEATH
OF HER MOTHER

Mourning in many ways is like falling in love. . . . All-consuming, blinding, it absents you from the world and absorbs you totally. . . . You seem to be filled with it. . . . In a sense, like pregnancy. But unlike the quickening of pregnancy, here a lead weight lodges in your stomach. Whereas pregnancy imparts a sense of doing something even while inactive, mourning bequeaths a sense of futility and meaninglessness in the midst of activity. . . . Her death is the only thing on my mind. . . . It is the only thing that counts.

Reduced, depleted, empty. I've no smile, no reflection, no shadow, no echo. I am stripped without her. Gone is that old sense of abundance, of surplus. Making, doing, anticipating, planning. Gone the desire to bake cake, preserve fruit, file clippings, press flowers, root plants, the impulse to hold, conserve, store. Camphoring clothes. For what? Let the moths get them. Why save empty jars for refilling, old notebooks for jottings, twists of string for future gifts, rubber bands?

. . . Now nothing seems worth saving. The rainy day has come, my savings are useless. Inconvertible currency. My mother epitomized my past, my present, my future. She encouraged me to save, to hope. To replenish old goose-down feathers with new, to sew fresh tickings, to wash grapes and ferment them in casks not too tightly sealed, to sort June strawberries and preserve them in vodka for February toddies. She sent me to the bank at age ten to open my first Christmas Club account, little weekly fifty-cent deposits which accrued into end-of-year bonanzas. As she said, you need bread to make a sandwich. But now my motion of preservation toward the future has died with her.

Even now, as I think of her, that familiar swelling constricts my throat, turns it into a lump of clay, which means I can cry. But in the throes of tears, memories inevitably get foreshortened. Reduced to freeze shots of her in the hospital, in the coffin. Then again, silently, incredulously, I have to begin from the beginning and repeat: She's dead. It's as if it's just struck me. And I find myself drowning, engulfed by the disorder of the current, wanting to seize her hand to bring me to shore. Missing her so. Futilely trying to recapture that profile of elusive contours and shapes. . . .

And then the idealization. . . . Idealizing her in a way antithetical to her nature. Bella was no lofty madonna, no enigmatic Mary, no *mater dolorosa*. She was a flesh-and-blood lady who got her hands wet, whose life encompassed pain and suffering. A human being with human flaws. It's a betrayal to remember only the good parts. Devoid of exertion, or resistance, or failure.

Bella identified herself primarily as a mother. This realization prompts me to reflect: Did I adequately repay her? Is my grief in part a sense of something owed her? What will I expect of my daughters when I am old?

What is it that I mourn? Her loss of life? The end of her pleasures? The fact that never again will she drink a glass of sweet country water, or bask in the sun, or set eyes upon her grandchildren, never again steep in a hot bath, or sip a cup of too hot coffee?

Or is it my own loss that I mourn? . . . The knowledge that she's in the next room, in the next house, in the next city. As when I was a child bedridden with a cold, knowing she was within reach of my voice, that I could bask in her calm, her vigilance and cheer. I could drift in and out of fevers and books and sleep and radio soap operas and cliff-hangers, and she'd still be there. Ready-at-hand.

Or perhaps I mourn the loss of my childhood and youth, of my past. I've lost the witness to my first tooth, my first haircut, my first period, my first bicycle lesson, my first boyfriend, my first fur coat, my first job, my first short story. . . . I mourn her record of me. Her support, her corroboration, her assurance that when things were bad, they'd get better.

Am I clinging to some youthful version of myself? Or is it my loss of innocence that I mourn? The knowledge that I have changed.

✳

Am I healing? I'm able to gaze at her photograph without that tourniquet tightening round my throat, clamping memory. Without hot tears flooding my eyes. I can hear her saying with a little smile: *Enough. Don't cry. Be a mensch! You have your life ahead of you.* Who was it that said: A mother is not to lean on, but to make leaning unnecessary?

✳

I remember so many things.

As a child, I'd sit on the edge of the tub on an evening when she was going out, watch her comb her hair and with her forefinger dab a bit of color on her lips. How good she smelled.

I remember how she straightened her dress, gripping its sides and giving a smart downward pull.

I remember her warming a bit of olive oil and rubbing it on my scalp with a ball of cotton to give sheen to my hair.

I remember how she'd encourage me, when nauseous, to stick two fingers into my mouth to vomit.

I remember when I had my tonsils out, awakening from the ether in a white iron hospital bed with bars at its side, my throat raw like an uprooted organ—and five teeth missing. The doctor had decided, while he had me under ether, to remove the loose baby teeth. My tongue slipped over the empty gaps. I felt doubly castrated. My mother cheered me. "Lucky girl, rid of your tonsils and ready for new teeth." She brought me vanilla ice cream.

I remember her pinching me in pique. Once she remarked that the shortest route away from trouble in the head is via the backside.

I remember her hemming my long yellow dotted-swiss prom dress. By eye. Making it uneven all the time, till that ankle-length gown wound up midi-length.

I remember her perennial question, "How can you sew without a thimble?"

My mother let go. I let her go. Yet always I am carrying her in me. Even find myself picking up some of her habits. This eternal attachment. Women—mothers. Daughters—mothers. The daughter leaves the mother. Separation, that essential task of adolescence, attended at times by anger, rebellions, rejections. Then rapprochement. Finally, the ultimate separation, the inevitable task of adulthood. Accompanied by numbness, hurt, anger. And then . . . what?

✺

. . . Since my mother's death I've been holding on, clinging desperately to her and to a youthful version of myself. Losing her physical being, her force, her umbrage, seemed a maiming, even an annihilation, of my own existence. She was the *mysterium tremendum* of life.

But that season is over.

Slowly I find myself being weaned from her material presence. Yet, filled with her as never before. It is I now who represent us both. I am our mutual past. I am my mother and my self. She gave me love, to love myself, and to love the world. I must remember how to love. . . .

She was the one who taught me to love and to receive love. To be unafraid. In her life and in the way she met death. My mother was at peace. She was ready. A free woman. "Let me go," she said. Okay, Mama. I'm letting you go.

The time has come to separate. For me to go back to the world alone.

Toby Talbot,
A Book About My Mother

It is the image in the mind that links us to our lost treasures; but it is the loss that shapes the image, gathers the flowers, weaves the garland.

Colette,
My Mother's House

GRIEVING A
SUICIDE OR
A SUDDEN DEATH

LIFE IN THE WAKE
OF A SUICIDE

Like a fatal heart attack, suicide is sudden, and like an automobile accident, it is violent; like death from cancer or AIDS, it marks the end of a long battle with pain. Suicide is all these things, and the suffering of the survivors is as intense, complex, and paradoxical as the act of self-destruction itself.

In one respect, suicide is unlike other deaths: it is a deliberate severance—the most profound act of disconnection that a human being can undertake—from one's own self and life, from others who have been part of that life, and from the human community. Suicide is an untimely chosen death, carried out alone and most often secretly. The isolation, secrecy, and disconnection of suicide become the survivors' legacy.

Perhaps the hardest and lowest point of grief that survivors experience in the wake of suicide is the feeling of powerlessness. Having struggled with questions of their own role in the death—how they failed and what they might have done to keep that person alive—they must finally come face to face with the limitations of their responsibility. In the end, we cannot keep another person alive; we cannot exercise that kind of power over another life, no matter how closely connected with it we are.

And yet, at the same time, we are responsible for our part in that connection. There is always something we might have done differently, but it might not have made a difference. We do and do not make a difference in other people's lives; we are both powerful and powerless. That is the paradox that suicide teaches us. It is a painful lesson but one that is also in some sense freeing. . . .

Life in the wake of suicide can be much more than simply a matter of functioning. As people find words and listeners for their grief, they move through it and gradually come to lead whole lives again. The "peculiar gift" of the journey is the knowledge that in one's very vulnerability to loss lies the strength to survive it and prosper.

Is it ever finished? Probably not. We cannot leave our losses behind; they stay within us, growing into our lives. But eventually *we* carry *them*—they no longer carry us. As time, like the tide, smooths their contours, we find a smaller, more comfortable place for them. Looking back, we can recognize the sea changes between then and now. . . .

Why should telling the story of a loss by suicide be so powerful? . . . By giving voice to their loss, by speaking of it out loud and being heard by others, the survivors break the secrecy and put an end to the silence. Perhaps most important, in the telling they begin to find a way of reconnecting—with both themselves and others.

> Victoria Alexander,
> in *Words I Never Thought to Speak: Stories of Life in the Wake of Suicide*

All I could think was, "If you want to *really* be a failure in life, have your child commit suicide." It's bad enough to lose a child and my heart really does go out to other bereaved parents, but the guilt you have over not getting them to a doctor "soon enough," the guilt over not being able to protect them from cancer or drunk drivers or whatever can't be as fundamental and soul-searing as knowing they couldn't endure the life you gave them.

Sue Chance,
Stronger Than Death: When Suicide Touches Your Life

. . . The stigma of self-inflicted death is for some people a hateful blot that demands erasure at all costs.

William Styron,
Darkness Visible: A Memoir of Madness

. . . Often every impulse in our psyche fights against [the work of grieving] because to learn from grief seems like sanctioning what has happened.

Martha Whitmore Hickman,
Healing After Loss

Get over the notion that it never makes sense, because it always makes sense to those who do it. They're just solving a problem, albeit in a way that creates a host of problems for those who are left behind. You can fault their logic all you like; you can point out that there were a plethora of other options they could have taken. But, recognize that they picked the option they did. *They* picked it, not you.

> Sue Chance,
> *Stronger Than Death: When*
> *Suicide Touches Your Life*

In both sudden death and anticipated death, there is pain. However, while the grief is not greater in sudden death, the capacity to cope is diminished. . . . if your loved one died suddenly, you may be unable to grasp the situation and find it difficult to understand the implications of the loss. . . .

You may find yourself looking back at the time leading up to the death and searching for clues that could have indicated what was to come. . . . This tendency to reconstruct events in your mind in order to allow for some anticipation of the death is quite common. It is an attempt to restructure what happened so that it seems you had some inkling that the death was going to occur. . . .

For survivors whose loved ones die suddenly, grief symptoms tend to persist longer. . . . You may feel a profound loss of security and confidence in the world. . . .

Your adaptive capabilities are seriously assaulted, and you suffer extreme feelings of bewilderment, anxiety, self-reproach, and depression . . . the death may continue to seem inexplicable. . . .

Therese A. Rando,
How to Go On Living When
Someone You Love Dies

There is but one serious philosophical problem and that is suicide. Judging whether life is or is not worth living amounts to answering the fundamental question of philosophy.

Albert Camus

HOUR OF GOLD, HOUR OF LEAD
THE KIDNAPPING AND MURDER
OF THE LINDBERGH BABY

[On] the evening of March 1, 1932, our eighteen-months-old child, Charles Lindbergh, Jr., was taken from his crib in our home near Hopewell, New Jersey, and a note was left on the window sill from the kidnapper demanding a ransom for his safe return. After ten weeks of negotiation and contact with the kidnapper and the handing over of the demanded ransom, the dead body of the child was found in the woods a few miles from our home. Newspapers of the time are full of accounts of the tragedy and books were written about the crime. In this period my diary reappears, and a series of letters to my mother-in-law, written almost daily after the kidnapping, give a full account of the progress of the case as we lived through it.

What needs to be explained are not outer facts but certain inner mysteries. How could I have written those letters which I have only recently recovered? I had not seen them since the day they were written. They were carefully put away among my mother-in-law's papers. When I first reread them, I was shocked and bewildered. How could I have been so self-controlled, so calm, so factual, in the midst of horror and suspense? And, above all, how could I have been so hopeful? Ten weeks of faithfully recorded details have the emotional unreality of hallucination. It was, of course, a nightmare, as my mother wrote at the time from Hopewell. "It changes but it is still a nightmare." The letters to my mother-in-law confirm the impression: "It is impossible to describe the confusion we are living in—a police station downstairs by day—detectives, police, secret service men swarming in and out—mattresses all over the dining room and other rooms at night. At any time I may be routed out of my bed so that a group of detectives may have a conference in the room. It is so terrifically unreal that I do not feel anything." Here is one key to the mystery.

Another key was hope. After the first shock, we were, to begin with, very hopeful for the safe return of the child. Everyone around us—friends, advisers, detectives, police—fed us hope, and it was this hope I tried to pass on to my mother-in-law. ("In a survey of 400 cities,

2000 kidnapped children returned." "Never in the history of crime has there been a case of a gang bargaining over a dead person.")

Not only was I surrounded by hopeful people, I was surrounded by disciplined people. The tradition of self-control and self-discipline was strong in my own family and also in that of my husband. The people around me were courageous and I was upheld by their courage. It was also necessary to be disciplined, not only for the safety of the child I was carrying but in order to work toward the safe return of the stolen child. As in war, or catastrophe, there was a job to be done. The job and hundreds of dedicated people working with us for the same end kept us going.

Also, as in war, the case, like a great bubbling cauldron of life itself, threw up both evil and good. Greed, madness, cruelty, and indifference were countered by goodness, devotion, self-sacrifice, and courage. There were people who fluttered around the flame of publicity, politicians who came and posed for pictures next to the kidnapper's ladder. There was one city official, acting as self-appointed investigator, who woke me in the middle of the night and asked me to re-enact his theory of the crime, which ended with the imaginary throwing of a baby into the furnace. And there were friends who left their homes and lives and slept on the floor of our house in order to help us. We were upheld by the devotion, loyalty, hopes, and prayers of many.

But after six weeks of unsuccessful efforts, after the ransom had been paid and no child was returned, after the clues began to run out, hope dwindled. I found it necessary, while trying to keep a surface composure for my husband, my family, and those working for and with us, to give way somewhere to the despair banked up within me. For sanity's sake I went back to writing in my diary, two days before the body of the child was found. . . .

🌤

I do not believe that sheer suffering teaches. If suffering alone taught, all the world would be wise, since everyone suffers. To suffering must be added mourning, understanding, patience, love, openness, and the willingness to remain vulnerable. All these and other factors combined, if the circumstances are right, *can* teach and *can* lead to rebirth.

But there is no simple formula, or swift way out, no comfort, or easy acceptance of suffering.

. . . Contrary to the general assumption, the first days of grief are not the worst. The immediate reaction is usually shock and numbing disbelief. One has undergone an amputation. After shock comes acute early grief which is a kind of "condensed presence"— almost a form of possession. One still feels the lost limb down to the nerve endings. It is as if the intensity of grief fused the distance between you and the dead. Or perhaps, in reality, part of one dies. Like Orpheus, one tries to follow the dead on the beginning of their journey. But one cannot, like Orpheus, go all the way, and after a long journey one comes back. If one is lucky, one is reborn. Some people die and are reborn many times in their lives. For others the ground is too barren and the time too short for rebirth. Part of the process is the growth of a new relationship with the dead, that *"véritable ami mort"* Saint-Exupéry speaks of. Like all gestation, it is a slow dark wordless process. While it is taking place one is painfully vulnerable. One must guard and protect the new life growing within—like a child.

One must grieve, and one must go through periods of numbness that are harder to bear than grief. One must refuse the easy escapes offered by habit and human tradition. The first and most common offerings of family and friends are always distractions ("Take her out"—"Get her away"—"Change the scene"—"Bring in people to cheer her up"—"Don't let her sit and mourn" [when it is mourning one needs]). On the other hand, there is the temptation to self-pity or glorification of grief. "I will instruct my sorrows to be proud," Constance cries in a magnificent speech in Shakespeare's *King John*. Despite her words, there is no aristocracy of grief. Grief is a great leveler. There is no highroad out.

Courage is a first step, but simply to bear the blow bravely is not enough. Stoicism is courageous, but it is only a halfway house on the long road. It is a shield, permissible for a short time only. In the end one has to discard shields and remain open and vulnerable. Otherwise, scar tissue will seal off the wound and no growth will follow. To grow, to be reborn, one must remain vulnerable—open to love but also hideously open to the possibility of more suffering.

Remorse is another dead end, a kind of fake action, the only kind that seems possible at the moment. It is beating oneself in a vain attempt to make what *has* happened "*un*-happen." ("If only I had done thus and so, it might not have been.") Remorse is fooling yourself, feeding on an illusion; just as living on memories, clinging to relics and photographs, is an illusion. Like the food offered one in dreams, it will not nourish; no growth or rebirth will come from it.

The inexorably difficult thing in life, and particularly in sorrow, is to face the truth. As Laurens Van der Post has written: "One of the most pathetic things about us human beings is our touching belief that there are times when the truth is not good enough for us; that it can and must be improved upon. We have to be utterly broken before we can realize that it is impossible to better the truth. It is the truth that we deny which so tenderly and forgivingly picks up the fragments and puts them together again."

Undoubtedly, the long road of suffering, insight, healing, or rebirth, is best illustrated in the Christian religion by the suffering, death, and resurrection of Christ. It is also illustrated by the story of Buddha's answer to a mother who had lost her child. According to the legend, he said that to be healed she needed only a mustard seed from a household that had never known sorrow. The woman journeyed from home to home over the world but never found a family ignorant of grief. Instead, in the paradoxical manner of myths and oracles, she found truth, understanding, compassion, and eventually, one feels sure, rebirth.

But when all is said about the universality of tragedy and the long way out, what can be added to human knowledge or insight by another example? I can only say that I could not bear to expose this story if I did not believe that one is helped by learning how other people come through their trials. Certainly I was strengthened by the personal experience of others. It is even helpful to learn the mistakes made. As the reader will see, I am familiar with the false roads: stoicism, pride, remorse, self-pity, clinging to scraps of memories. I have not named them all; they are legion. I tried most of them. The fact that, in our case, horror was added to suffering does not change its fundamental character. The overlay of crime, horror, or accident on loss *does* increase suffering, but chiefly, I have come to feel, because it delays healing. It separates one from "the long way out," the normal process of mourning, of facing reality, of remaining open, and of eventual rebirth. . . .

It isn't for the moment you are struck that you need courage but for the long uphill climb back to sanity and faith and security.

Anne Morrow Lindbergh,
Hour of Gold, Hour of Lead

Till Death Us Do Part (Widows and Widowers)

To have and to hold from this day forward, for better, for worse, for richer, for poorer, in sickness and in health, to love and to cherish till death us do part.

The Book of Common Prayer

For two years . . . I was just as crazy as you can be and still be at large. I didn't have any really normal minutes during those two years. It wasn't just grief. It was total confusion. I was nutty, and that's the truth. How did I come out of it? I don't know, because I didn't know when I was in it that I was in it.

Helen Hayes, the actress, on the death of her husband Charles MacArthur

The most I ever did for you, was to outlive you But that is much.

Edna St. Vincent Millay

They say it is only the possibility of committing suicide that keeps grief-stricken people from going mad. It's absolutely true. In the moments of terrible total despair, there has to be an alternative to those awful words that haunt—

> Forever
> Never again
> Alone
> I'm fine.

> Anne M. Brooks,
> *The Grieving Time*

I finally saw what depression is. I finally saw the edge of the cliff. I always knew there was a point where people can't stand it anymore. They go crazy or they kill themselves or they slip into some unreachable place. I'd never had a personal sense of that unreachable place, but for the first time in my life, I was able to see it. There were moments when I could see it. Suddenly there's this huge hollow space that swallows you up. And it's very very hard to get back from. You lose your hold.

I'm not sure I have completely pulled back from the edge of that cliff yet. I think a lot of it had to do with the anticipation of the anniversary of Joanne's death, that I was attaching something to that. That somehow I didn't want to let go. Didn't *want* to get beyond it. Because Joanne's death, her illness and death, had been the most important thing that I had ever done—the most difficult, the most challenging, the most important thing that I had ever done in my life. And there I was. It was over. And mundanity was setting in. While she was sick, it was there every day, that sense of urgency. And I could put aside my stupid job at the newspaper. I could go in and put in my eight hours a day, but my real job was with Joanne. Nothing will be that urgent again. That's all gone now. And I haven't found anything nearly as satisfying, nearly as fulfilling, nearly as important.

> From *Widower,*
> by Scott Campbell with Phyllis
> R. Silverman

From We to I

In conversation, I am accustomed to saying "our," as in, "our" garden and "our" living room. I find myself continuing to use the plural, catching myself, changing it to the singular, and then muttering, "Well, you know what I mean," to the person I am speaking to.

I note that I mention Bill's name as many times a day as possible. Retelling one of his anecdotes, referring to his thinking on an issue, pointing to his expertise and wise counsel, recounting a story that casts him in what I always see as an omniscient light, makes me feel closer to him. I imagine that this is tedious to a number of people, but I cannot stop myself.

I have taken to using phrases that are Bill's phrases, not mine. When people inquire after my welfare, I am at a

loss for words. In the past, my rote response would have
been, "Just fine, thanks," or sometimes, even,
"Couldn't be better." Dissembling has never been one
of my strong suits, but now I adopt Bill's phrase, the one
he used almost up until the end: "Not bad," I now say to
most who ask. My close friends don't need to ask. They
know that I am close to catatonic.

❧❦

"When do you figure you're going to get back your old
personality?" an extremely dear and valued friend asks
me. This is a woman, a sensitive one at that, who along
with a handful of other friends has carefully watched me
as I try to manage the unmanageable. . . .

"Never," I say, struggling hard to think back to what
my old personality was, or at least to what my old personality was perceived to be. Whatever it was, I feel as
far removed from it as I do from Tokyo, where I have
never been.

"Maybe someday I'll be a version of the person I once
was," I tell this woman for whom I have boundless affection but now wonder if I should, "but I think I have to
tell you that it is impossible to watch your husband die
for ten months and then think that you will ever be the
same again. Ever."

No one can tell you about grief, about its limitless
boundaries, its unfathomable depths. No one can tell you
about the crater that is created in the center of your
body, the one that nothing can fill. No matter how many
times you hear the word *final*, it means nothing until final
is actually final. . . .

And as far as I can tell there is only one certainty, a certainty that is as solid as the realization that he is dead, and it is the sure knowledge that I have now learned, am continuing to learn, another language, the language of loss. Like the language of music and love, it is universal. You don't need a dictionary, you don't need a translator, you don't need a thesaurus.

All you need do is go through it once, just once, to get it. Bereavement. Grief. Sorrow. Mourning. Devastation. Loss. Despair. The books or newspaper articles you read or the advice you are given will or will not help you. What I have come to know is that you do what you have to do to go on. Some people will call it surviving, but you will know that it is a matter of just going on. You do what you are capable of, you do what you think will cause the least amount of pain. To yourself and to others.

. . . I do not turn on the radio, because I cannot decide which is worse: the thundering sound of silence that envelops me night and day or the reminder that it was Bill's habit to play the radio at all times, while he was shaving or showering or writing or reading.

There is not a second in the day that I do not long to hear his voice, listen to his advice, yearn to hear the laugh that made everyone around him smile. It is not possible for me to envision a life without him, and I know with a frightening surety that I will not be able to get along now.

I am using his toothbrush and his comb. I am wearing his shirts, their very largeness a small comfort in a universe in which comfort has been swept away. I am wearing his wedding ring, inscribed with the initials RLW, RUTH

LOVES WILLIAM, on the middle finger of my left hand, right next to my own wedding ring, which I cannot contemplate ever removing.

At home, the house becomes a memorial to Bill, with photographs of him everywhere. Since his death, I have brought out more pictures and have had them framed, have added them to the walls and to the tops of tables. The experts call it enshrinement. I call it keeping him close.

"What is this," someone asks me, horror evident in her voice, "are you constructing some kind of monument here?" I am affronted by this question, even as I know how bizarre this must look to the outsider, the uninitiated; even as I know that I am turning into a modern-day Miss Havisham, the difference being, of course, that Miss Havisham was captured, frozen in time, waiting for her bridegroom on the wedding day that never took place and that I am captured, frozen in time, on the day that did take place, the day my husband died.

. . . It is impossible to stop the videotape that continues to play in your mind, the months, the weeks, the last days, the last hours, the last minutes, in full color.

To imply that I am oblivious to the needs of others would be neither fair nor accurate, and it is true, too, that I often think how horrible it would be to see my friends go through this. But I am acutely aware of how self-centered in this whirlpool of despair I have become. There are moments, for instance, when I would like to tell people that until you experience a loss this big, everything else is amateur night.

It is what I have come to call the dwarfing down of

reality, the difference between an oak and a bonsai, the unassailable evidence that, compared to death and devastation, the rest of what passes for ordinary life is small change.

People have spoken to me about my lack of preparation, arguing that since I knew Bill was going to die, I should have been ready for it, less shocked, more serene. There is no such thing as preparation, I counter; while he was dying, it was all I could do to take care of him. Envisioning life without him was beyond my reach; you can't exactly liken the ten months of his illness to a fire drill and his death to the actual fire.

Ruth Coughlin,
Grieving: A Love Story

Strength In Numbers

I had my gun in my mouth, when suddenly something dawned on me. I had my wife's dog to take care of. Ginger. She was living in the backyard. I hadn't been thinking about Ginger. But suddenly I realized I couldn't leave that dog to starve. I'd have to kill the dog. And that I could not do. So I put the gun down. I decided if Ginger died, *then* I would kill myself. But she didn't die; she's still alive. And it turned out that having that dog to care for was a helpful thing. You have to feed them, give them water, walk them, stuff like that. And it has to be done regularly. It kept me surviving for a while.

Years before, I had clipped a story out of the newspa-

per called "How To Survive the Death of Your Spouse."
At that time, I didn't know if Angie was going to die for
sure, but I saved it so either she or I would be able to use
it. And now I was desperate for help. So I called the
Widowed Persons Service in Washington, D.C.—their
number was in that article—and they were kind enough
to give me the number of someone out here. That person
was no longer involved, but they found somebody who
was, and they in turn put me in contact with a volunteer
aid. And that person saved my life. We talked, and for
the first time . . .

See, I literally had no friends. When my wife got sick,
I became more or less isolated because she needed
twenty-four-hour-a-day care. And when I came out here,
of course, I was a complete stranger. It turned out my
son was out of town for a good part of the year, so I
hardly ever saw him. I tried to talk to him once, early on,
but it didn't work very well. Later, I found a cartoon and
I told him, This is what your help was like. The cartoon
was a picture of a man on a psychiatrist's couch and the
psychiatrist is flailing his arms and saying, "Pack up your
troubles in your old kit bag and Smile! Smile! Smile!"
My son didn't know how to react to it. He laughed. I
think he realized that that was all he could do, he didn't
know what I was going through. And I didn't know what
was happening with him, you know, grieving for his
mother. We were just a pair of human beings trying to
find our way. But after that one attempt with him, I
talked to no one, really.

What this volunteer aid did for me was to allow me to
tell somebody what I was going through, and that was the

beginning of identifying what I'd lost. You can't just say that you lost a spouse, that's not saying enough. You've lost a lot of things. You've lost a companion, an ego builder, you've lost a counsellor who will tell you when you're right or when you're wrong. You've lost all of that. And you have to name what you've lost. I was also retired, and retirement is a loss to grieve too. When I first retired, I was so busy caring for my wife that it didn't really sink in. But when I got to Santa Barbara, it did sink in that I had also lost part of my identity. I was just a bum with money. At least I was a bum with money. Thank goodness I had enough of that.

We met in a public place, on the street, this volunteer aid and I. I was afraid of meeting someone like that, to tell you the truth. I didn't really know what this organization was all about. But we met and had lunch, and that was when my recovery started. Eventually, we had several conversations, always alone, nine or ten times, over a period of six months. We talked about problems of widowhood, such as, what do you do with this feeling that if I had done just one more thing . . . ? And it worked just like the Widowed Persons Service wants it to work. You're with them, they help you for a while, and then they up and leave you. I always call it—these days, when I do it—I say, I love them and leave them. You don't want to stay around and develop a dependency state.

This experience got me interested in the Widowed Persons Service, and I took the training class so I could be a volunteer aid myself. Telling your story is part of the class, so I had to tell my story to people so they could tell their story to me. And that's how I started to talk to people. And it was just astonishing, the way my attitude changed. My depression just went away. It was a miracle. And it all came from telling the story, and talking with other people in the same boat.

✹

. . . I'm still kind of taken aback when I think of all I did that first year. It just sort of bowls me over. My experience with other grieving people through the Widowed Persons Service—I'd be surprised to see somebody moving along that quick. But I wasn't running from my grief, because I was expressing it through this monthly support group meeting. That made me aware of the need to express it and to look into it—the term we use is ''lean into the pain.''

from *Widower,*
by Scott Campbell with Phyllis
R. Silverman

Western wind, when wilt thou blow,
   The small rain down can rain?
Christ, if my love were in my arms
   And I in my bed again!

Anonymous

WHEN FRIENDS BECOME
ACQUAINTANCES

The metamorphosis of married friends into acquaintances takes time and at first is not very noticeable. At first it is a matter of the phone not ringing as often with reports on bargain shopping, requests for your lemon-pie recipe. All this was perfectly understandable since I was mostly at work, but after a while, when I noticed that my party dresses hadn't been off the hangers in months, I was frightened. Love is a gift you may or may not keep, but friendship, we are promised, endures. Did those party dresses have sisters in the closets of other single women all over town, or was I, having become too different, too thorny, the only one not seeing the insides of my friends' houses after dark? . . .

Sundays were the worst. Sundays my friends were incommunicado, turned inward toward families. Each Sunday I read the funny papers in careful detail, took a swim and a long walk with Katie, ate a peanut-butter sandwich and tried to figure what to do with the rest of the day. I became a Sunday matinee movie fan, especially on three-day weekends. They were a necklace of terrible Sundays strung together.

"You mustn't join the widows' club," said Booth when he knew he was going to die and I was still refusing to believe it. I brushed it away then. He wasn't going to die. I wouldn't let him. Now, over the weekends, I wondered what other widows did. . . .

Christmas, if you're alone, is Sunday to the nth power, and all the holes in the life you put together for yourself become glaringly apparent. The papers are always full of people who realize on Christmas that it isn't worthwhile going on alone. Christmas by yourself would be even worse than your birthday alone, because the rules say at Christmas *everybody* has to be happy. Children may have been invented to come home at Christmas and take care of this lost feeling. . . .

> Elizabeth C. Mooney,
> *Alone: Surviving as a Widow*

Chances are, once you've gone through this, you'll never again watch Greta Garbo's death scene in "Camille" without wondering if Robert Taylor had joint tenancy with right of survivorship.

> Patricia Anderson,
> from *Affairs in Order*

A Different Woman

In my grief, my loneliness, and my panic, I became utterly self-absorbed and self-pitying, locked into myself and my misery. And I was scared—I was so scared my fear immobilized me. If my mother had not stayed with us for more than a year, I don't know how my children would have survived. Jonny and Buffy had lost not only their father, they had lost their mother too. For months, quivering with my own hurt, I was oblivious to theirs.

I was constantly tired. I would come home from work bone weary, and by the time the children were in bed, I was trembling with fatigue. Then I began waking up terrified at three and four in the morning. I learned that it helped to get up and make myself a cup of tea with honey. I would get back in bed with a pad of lined yellow paper and write. Some of the things I wrote were so vile that I burned them so the children would never read them. I wrote about my fears, my anger, my loneliness, my obsession with money, my problems with the children. I called the yellow pads my "paper psychiatrist," and writing proved to be good therapy. Putting my worries down on paper made them easier to think about; spelling them out made them less terrifying. I began to learn about myself.

Slowly, I emerged from the abyss of terror. I lived through the seasons of grief, none of which can be denied if we are to emerge on its other side. I began to accept responsibility for my own life, and there came a day when I realized that I was a stronger woman than I had been, that I was another woman now, and that I liked this woman better.

Lynn Caine,
Lifelines

The truth is that by and large, no matter how calm and controlled and accepting a face she may present to the world, a new widow is miserable and can be a very difficult creature.

What else could she be? The most important person in her life is no longer there. She has lost the love and companionship of the person with whom she has shared much of her life. She has lost status, both social and economic. She has lost her future.

Joyce Brothers,
Widowed

Most of us, unless we are the exception, outlive the men we marry. It is a probability built into every marriage vow, the specter at the wedding feast and something of which we choose not to think. We tend to marry men older than we, and then of course women are simply tougher. The years alone are slated before we begin.

But oddly, there are compensations. You cannot imagine that this can be true in the beginning, but it is as true as that Tuesday follows Monday and that, barring catastrophe, spring comes around again every year. I ask and I listen when I meet other women who have lost the men they loved, and I know that this is true.

We compromise and we learn to cope, we widows, and in the end we are different women, stronger women, women who come to respect ourselves. It is the gift that comes after the fire.

Elizabeth C. Mooney,
Alone: Surviving as a Widow

To spare oneself from grief at all cost can be achieved only at the price of total detachment, which excludes the ability to experience happiness.

Erich Fromm

HABITS REMEMBERED, TENDERLY

Are we both widowers within six months? Marriage is a mystery even when, like mine, it is effected by a registrar (we neither of us could stand the Church of England service). I suppose every marriage is different: some are failures and never consummate themselves except physically, which means that they are not human marriages at all. I don't know why you did not live with Olive; her treating you badly (as I do) has nothing to do with it; all couples who live together treat each other badly occasionally, and treat third parties very well. But the relationship is unique and mysterious. I have known women with whom I could get on with less friction than with Charlotte; but their deaths have not affected me in the same way. Her ashes are preserved at Golders Green, and my instructions are that mine are to be inseparably mixed with them, after which they may be scattered to the winds or immured in Westminster Abbey for all I care. When I come across something intimate of her belongings I have a welling of emotion and quite automatically say something endearing to her. But I am not in the least desolate; on the contrary I am enjoying my solitude and have improved markedly in health since her

death set me free. But you, who lived alone, feel desolate. There is no logic in it: it is a mystery.

> George Bernard Shaw,
> quoted in a letter to Alfred
> Douglas, 1944

Habit is not mere subjugation, it is a tender tie; when
one remembers habit it seems to have been happiness.

> Elizabeth Bowen

DEATH AND WIDOWHOOD

One final word to my contemporaries. Take time to plan
your future. Do not let your relatives or friends, anxious
for your welfare, push you into some hasty move that
later you may regret. If it is financially possible for you,
stay in your own home, with the familiar things about
you. We need many months to become reconciled to the
loss that has overtaken us; and if at first the silence of the
empty house may seem unbearable, do not forget it is
still the home you shared, which two persons made their
own.

As the months pass and the seasons change, something
of tranquillity descends, and although the well-remem-
bered footstep will not sound again, nor the voice call
from the room beyond, there seems to be about one in
the air an atmosphere of love, a living presence. I say this
in no haunting sense, ghosts and phantoms are far from

my mind. It is as though one shared, in some indefinable manner, the freedom and the peace, even at times the joy, of another world where there is no more pain. It is not a question of faith or of belief. It is not necessary to be a follower of any religious doctrine to become aware of what I mean. It is not the prerogative of the devout. The feeling is simply there, pervading all thought, all action. When Christ the healer said, "Blessed are they that mourn, for they shall be comforted," he must have meant just this.

Later, if you go away, if you travel, even if you decide to make your home elsewhere, the spirit of tenderness, of love, will not desert you. You will find that it has become part of you, rising from within yourself; and because of it you are no longer fearful of loneliness, of the dark, because death, the last enemy, has been overcome.

Daphne du Maurier

Love is not changed by Death,
And nothing is lost and all in the end is harvest.

Dame Edith Sitwell,
"Eurydice"

A GRIEF OBSERVED

The film Shadowlands *portrays the marriage in the 1950s of an American woman, Joy Davidman Gresham, to C. S. Lewis, an Oxford don and up to that point a lifelong bachelor. After three very happy years, Joy Gresham (H. in the passages below) died from cancer. Lewis worked through his grief by recording it in a journal, which was later published as* A Grief Observed. *The following excerpts from that classic journal have resonated equally for men and women.*

No one ever told me that grief felt so like fear. I am not afraid, but the sensation is like being afraid. The same fluttering in the stomach, the same restlessness, the yawning. I keep on swallowing.

At other times it feels like being mildly drunk, or concussed. There is a sort of invisible blanket between the world and me. I find it hard to take in what anyone says. Or perhaps, hard to want to take it in. It is so uninteresting. Yet I want the others to be about me. I dread the moments when the house is empty. If only they would talk to one another and not to me.

There are moments, most unexpectedly, when something inside me tries to assure me that I don't really mind so much, not so very much, after all. Love is not the whole of a man's life. I was happy before I ever met H. I've plenty of what are called "resources." People get over these things. Come, I shan't do so badly. One is ashamed to listen to this voice but it seems for a little to be making out a good case. Then comes a sudden jab of red-hot memory and all this "common-sense" vanishes like an ant in the mouth of a furnace. . . .

And no one ever told me about the laziness of grief. Except at my job—where the machine seems to run on much as usual—I loathe the slightest effort. Not only writing but even reading a letter is too much. Even shaving. . . . It's easy to see why the lonely become untidy; finally, dirty and disgusting. . . .

. . . An odd by-product of my loss is that I'm aware of being an embarrassment to everyone I meet. At work, at the club, in the street, I see people, as they approach me, trying to make up their minds whether they'll "say something about it" or not. I hate it if they do, and if they don't. . . . Perhaps the bereaved ought to be isolated in special settlements like lepers.

To some I'm worse than an embarrassment. I am a death's head. Whenever I meet a happily married pair I can feel them both thinking, "One or other of us must some day be as he is now."

. . . Already, less than a month after her death, I can feel the slow, insidious beginning of a process that will make the H. I think of into a more and more imaginary woman. Founded on fact, no doubt. I shall put in nothing fictitious (or I hope I shan't). But won't the composition inevitably become more and more my own? The reality is no longer there to check me, to pull me up short, as the real H. so often did, so unexpectedly, by being so thoroughly herself and not me.

. . . Something quite unexpected has happened. It came this morning early. For various reasons, not in themselves at all mysterious, my heart was lighter than it had been for many weeks. For one thing, I suppose I am recovering physically from a good deal of mere exhaustion. And I'd had a very tiring but very healthy twelve hours the day before, and a sounder night's sleep; and after ten days of low-hung gray skies and motionless warm dampness, the sun was shining and there was a light breeze. And suddenly at the very moment when, so far, I mourned H. least, I remembered her best. Indeed it was something (almost) better than memory; an instantaneous, unanswerable impression. To say it was like a meeting would be going too far. Yet there was that in it which tempts one to use those words. It was as if the lifting of the sorrow removed a barrier.

Why has no one told me these things? How easily I might have misjudged another man in the same situation? I might have said, "He's got over it. He's forgotten his wife," when the truth was, "He remembers her better *because* he has partly got over it."

. . . I think I am beginning to understand why grief feels like suspense. It comes from the frustration of so many impulses that had become habitual. Thought after thought, feeling after feeling, action after action, had H. for their object. Now their target is gone. I keep on through habit fitting an arrow to the string; then I remember and have to lay the bow down. So many roads lead thought to H. I set out on one of them. But now there's an impassable frontier-post across it. So many roads once; now so many *culs de sac*.

Still, there's no denying that in some sense I "feel better," and with that comes at once a sort of shame, and a feeling that one is under a sort of obligation to cherish and foment and prolong one's unhappiness. I've read about that in books, but I never dreamed I should feel it myself. I am sure H. wouldn't approve of it. She'd tell me not to be a fool. So I'm pretty certain, would God. What is behind it?

. . . For me at any rate the program is plain. I will turn to her as often as possible in gladness. I will even salute her with a laugh. The less I mourn her the nearer I seem to her.

An admirable program. Unfortunately it can't be carried out. Tonight all the hells of young grief have opened again; the mad words, the bitter resentment, the fluttering in the stomach, the nightmare unreality, the wallowed-in tears. For in grief nothing "stays put." One keeps on emerging from a phase, but it always recurs. Round and round. Everything repeats. Am I going in circles, or dare I hope I am on a spiral?

But if a spiral, am I going up or down it?

. . . I thought I could describe a *state;* make a map of sorrow. Sorrow, however, turns out to be not a state but a process. It needs not a map but a history, and if I don't stop writing that history at some quite arbitrary point, there's no reason why I should ever stop. There is something new to be chronicled every day. Grief is like a long valley, a winding valley where any bend may reveal a totally new landscape. As I've already noted, not every bend does. Sometimes the surprise is the opposite one; you are presented with exactly the same sort of country

you thought you had left behind miles ago. That is when
you wonder whether the valley isn't a circular trench.
But it isn't. There are partial recurrences, but the sequence doesn't repeat.

C. S. Lewis,
excerpted from *A Grief Observed*

Looking down into my father's
dead face
for the last time
my mother said without
tears, without smiles
without regrets
but with *civility*
"Goodnight, Willie Lee, I'll see you
in the morning."
And it was then I knew that the healing
of all our wounds
is forgiveness
that permits a promise
of our return
at the end.

Alice Walker,
"Goodnight, Willie Lee, I'll
See You in the Morning"

Death is nothing at all. It does not count. I have only slipped away into the next room. Nothing has happened. Everything remains exactly as it was. I am I, and you are you, and the old life that we lived so fondly together is untouched, unchanged. Whatever we were to each other, that we are still. Call me by the old familiar name. Speak of me in the easy way which you always used. Put no difference into your tone. Wear no forced air of solemnity or sorrow. Laugh as we always laughed at the little jokes that we enjoyed together. Play, smile, think of me, pray for me. Let my name be ever the household word that it always was. Let it be spoken without an effort, without the ghost of a shadow upon it. Life means all that it ever meant. It is the same as it ever was. There is absolute and unbroken continuity. What is death but a negligible accident? Why should I be out of mind because I am out of sight? I am but waiting for you, for an interval, somewhere very near, just around the corner. All is well.

> Henry Scott Holland,
> quoted by Rosamunde Pilcher
> in the novel *September*

Life is eternal; and love is immortal; and death is only a horizon; and a horizon is nothing save the limit of our sight.

> Rossiter Worthington Raymond

Seventeen years ago you said
   Something that sounded like Goodbye;
   And everybody thinks that you are dead,
    But I.
So I, as I grow stiff and cold
   To this and that say Goodbye too;
   And everybody sees that I am old
    But you.
   And one fine morning in a sunny lane
Some boy and girl will meet and kiss and swear
   That nobody can love their way again,
    While over there
You will have smiled, I shall have tossed your hair.

             Charlotte Mew

REMEMBER ME

GRIEF RITUALS

Grief rituals help us both say good-bye to and remember our loved ones in loving, healing ways and with a sense of peace. It is important to create a ritual that will have meaning to you and those you love, including the person who has died. Too often, we feel we must "hold on" to pain, seemingly forever, to remember those we love. Sometimes, to encourage your tears and love to flow, it helps to hold a memorial service, a gathering of friends and family to share tender, funny, painful, and typical stories and final thoughts about the person who has died. If the weather is good enough to hold at least part of the service outdoors, each of you might hold a balloon on a string; when you've finished, release the balloon as a symbol of letting go, of releasing the spirit. Here are some grief rituals that have worked for other people:

• Create a memory book, a scrapbook of memories and photos.

• At a family "memory" evening, share pictures, reminisce about special times, create or share a memory book, and so on. Do the sort of thing that person loved to do.

• Donate gifts or offer a scholarship in the name of your loved one.

• On birthdays, anniversaries, or holidays, buy your loved one a gift and donate it to a hospital or nursing home.

• For someone who has died of AIDS, make a quilt for the Names Project Quilt (contact the Names Project Foundation, 310 Townsend St., San Francisco, CA 94107).

• Help feed the hungry and homeless on holidays (by helping others you step outside yourself, and some of the misery dissipates).

• Plant a strong, healthy tree or flowering plant in the loved one's name.

• Find a tree in the canyons or woods, tie a yellow ribbon around it, and go there often to remember. (This is especially helpful when ashes have been scattered and there is no gravesite.)

• Buy a special Christmas ornament each year to add to your tree and remind you of them.

• Buy a special candle and light it at special times, such as birthdays, anniversaries, father's day, or the anniversary of their death.

• Have your wedding ring melted down and redesigned as a pin or the pendant in a necklace.

- Have a party on their birthday, playing their favorite music.

- If you go on a trip at a special anniversary time, do something special on the trip as a remembrance (toss a rose in the ocean, for example, or light a candle).

> Adapted from a course
> handbook of Kathleen Braza

Remember me when I am gone away,
   Gone far away into the silent land;
   When you can no more hold me by the hand,
Nor I half turn to go yet turning stay.
Remember me when no more day by day
   You tell me of our future that you planned:
   Only remember me; you understand
It will be late to counsel then or pray.
Yet if you should forget me for a while
   And afterwards remember, do not grieve:
   For if the darkness and corruption leave
   A vestige of the thoughts that once I had,
Better by far you should forget and smile
   Than that you should remember and be sad.

> Christina Rossetti,
> "Remember"

Scatter my ashes in my garden
so I can be near my loves.
Say a few honest words, sing a gentle song,
join hands in a circle of flesh.
Please tell some stories about me
making you laugh. I love to make you laugh.
When I've had time to settle, and green
gathers into buds, remember I love blossoms
bursting in spring. As the season ripens
remember my persistent passion.
And if you come in my garden
on an August afternoon
pluck a bright red globe,
let juice run down your chin and the seeds
stick to your cheek. When I'm dead
I want folks to smile and say *That Patti,*
she sure is some tomato!

> Patti Tana,
> "Post Humus"

If I should go before the rest of you,
Break not a flower nor inscribe a stone.
Nor when I'm gone speak in a Sunday voice,
But be the usual selves that I have known.
Weep if you must,
Parting is hell,
But life goes on,
So sing as well.

> Joyce Grenfell,
> "The First to Go"

Under the wide and starry sky,
Dig the grave and let me lie.
Glad did I live and gladly die,
    And I laid me down with a will.

This be the verse you grave for me:
Here he lies where he longed to be;
Home is the sailor, home from sea,
    And the hunter home from the hill.

> Robert Louis Stevenson,
> "Requiem" (his own epitaph)

I have fought a good fight. I have finished my course. I have kept the faith.

> Paul's Epistle to Timothy

As you love me, let there be
No mourning when I go—
No tearful eyes, no hopeless sighs.
No woe, nor even sadness.
Indeed, I would not have you sad.
For I myself shall be full glad
With the high triumphant gladness
Of a soul made free
Of God's sweet liberty.
No windows darkened, for my own
Will be flung wide, as ne'er before.
To catch the radiant in-pour
Of Love that shall in full atone
For all the ills that I have done.
No voices hushed: my own, full-flushed
With an immortal hope, will rise
In ecstasies of new-born bliss
And joyful melodies.
Rather, of your sweet courtesy
Rejoice with me
At my soul's loosing from captivity.
Wish me 'Bon Voyage' as you do a friend
Whose joyous visit finds its happy end
And bid me both 'Adieu' and 'Au revoir'
Since, though I come no more
I shall be waiting there to greet you
At His door.

And, as the feet of the bearers tread
The ways I trod.
Think not of me as dead, but rather—

Happy, thrice happy, he whose course is sped
He has gone home—to God.
His Father.

> John Oxenham,
> "Adieu and Au Revoir"

When I am dead, my dearest,
  Sing no sad songs for me;
Plant thou no roses at my head,
  Nor shady cypress tree:
Be the green grass above me
  With showers and dewdrops wet;
And if thou wilt, remember,
  And if thou wilt, forget.

I shall not see the shadows,
  I shall not feel the rain;
I shall not hear the nightingale
  Sing on as if in pain:
And dreaming through the twilight
  That doth not rise nor set,
Haply I may remember,
  And haply may forget.

> Christina Rossetti,
> "Song"

Sing me a song,
A canticle of life,
For I am leaving land
And taking space to wife.

Into the rising wind
I'll shout the ecstasy,
Echoes will answer back,
I am where I wished to be.

Winifred R. Lewis

Do not stand at my grave and weep;
I am not there. I do not sleep.
I am a thousand winds that blow.
I am the diamond glints on snow.
I am the sunlight on ripened grain.
I am the gentle autumn's rain.
When you awaken in the morning's hush,
I am the swift uplifting rush
Of quiet birds in circled flight.
I am the soft stars that shine at night.
Do not stand at my grave and cry;
I am not there. I did not die.

Anonymous

To live in hearts we leave behind,
Is not to die.

Thomas Campbell,
"Hallowed Ground"

MORE THOUGHTS
ON LIFE
AND DEATH

In the following poem, the speaker stands before a painting by Pieter Breughel of Icarus, a popular figure from mythology. Using wings his father Daedalus had made of feathers and wax, Icarus flies too close to the sun; the wax melts, and he falls into the sea.

About suffering they were never wrong,
The Old Masters: how well they understood
Its human position; how it takes place
While someone else is eating or opening a window or
    just walking dully along;
How, when the aged are reverently, passionately
    waiting
For the miraculous birth, there always must be
Children who did not specially want it to happen,
    skating
On a pond at the edge of the wood:
They never forgot
That even the dreadful martyrdom must run its course
Anyhow in a corner, some untidy spot
Where the dogs go on with their doggy life and the
    torturer's horse
Scratches its innocent behind on a tree.

In Brueghel's *Icarus,* for instance: how everything turns
    away
Quite leisurely from the disaster, the ploughman may
Have heard the splash, the forsaken cry,
But for him it was not an important failure; the sun
    shone
As it had to on the white legs disappearing into the
    green
Water; and the expensive delicate ship that must have
    seen
Something amazing, a boy falling out of the sky,
Had somewhere to get to and sailed calmly on.

> W. H. Auden,
> "Musée des Beaux Arts"

The sorrows of humanity are no one's sorrows. . . . A
thousand people drowned in floods in China are news; a
solitary child drowned in a pond is tragedy.

> Josephine Tey, *The Daughter of
> Time*

It is a sad weakness in us, after all, that the thought of a
man's death hallows him anew to us; as if life were not
sacred, too.

> George Eliot

We look on those approaching the banks of a river all must cross, with ten times the interest they excited when dancing in the meadow.

Hester Lynch Piozzi

It is as natural to die as to be born; and to a little infant, perhaps, the one is as painful as the other.

Sir Francis Bacon

The obituary pages tell us of the news that we are dying away; while the birth announcements in finer print, off at the side of the page, inform us of our replacements, but we get no grasp from this of the enormity of scale. There are 3 billion of us on the earth, and all 3 billion must be dead, on a schedule, within this lifetime. The vast mortality, involving something over 50 million of us each year, takes place in relative secrecy. We can only really know of the deaths in our households, or among our friends. These, detached in our minds from all the rest, we take to be unnatural events, anomalies, outrages. We speak of our own dead in low voices; struck down, we say, as though visible death can only occur for cause, by disease or violence, avoidably. . . .

Less than a half century from now, our replacements will have more than doubled the numbers. It is hard to see how we can continue to keep the secret, with such multitudes doing the dying. We will have to give up the notion that death is catastrophe, or detestable, or avoidable, or even strange. We will need to learn more about the cycling of life in the rest of the system, and about our connection to the process. Everything that comes alive seems to be in trade for something that dies, cell for cell.

Lewis Thomas,
The Lives of a Cell

We feel close to each other when we see ourselves as strangers and outsiders on this planet or see the planet as an island of life in a dark immensity of nothingness. We also draw together when we are aware that night must close in on all living things; that we are condemned to death at birth; and that life is a bus ride to the place of execution. All our squabbling and vying about seats in the bus, and the ride is over before we know it.

Eric Hoffer,
In Our Time

Every blade in the field—
   Every leaf in the forest—
Lays down its life
   in its season
as beautifully
as it was taken up.

Henry David Thoreau

It is impossible that anything so natural, so necessary, and so universal as death, should ever have been designed by Providence as an evil to mankind.

Jonathan Swift

Your death is a part of the order of the universe, 'tis a part of the life of the world . . . Give place to others, as others have given place to you.

Michel de Montaigne

No thought exists in me which death has not carved with his chisel.

Michelangelo

I acquired more wealth, power and prestige than most. But you can acquire all you want and still feel empty. What power wouldn't I trade for a little more time with my family? What price wouldn't I pay for an evening with friends? It took a deadly illness to put me eye to eye with that truth, but it is a truth that the country, caught up in its ruthless ambitions, can learn on my dime.

Lee Atwater,
former chairman of the
National Republican
Committee, as he lay dying of
brain cancer

This poem about life as a voyage of discovery is often read at memorial services. Maurice Tempelsman read it at the funeral mass for Jacqueline Kennedy Onassis in May 1994.

When you set out for Ithaka
pray that your road's a long one,
full of adventure, full of discovery.
Laistrygonians, Cyclops,
angry Poseidon—don't be scared of them:
you won't find things like that on your way
as long as your thoughts are exalted,
as long as a rare excitement
stirs your spirit and your body.
Laistrygonians, Cyclops,
wild Poseidon—you won't encounter them
unless you bring them along inside you,
unless your soul raises them up in front of you.

Pray that your road's a long one.
May there be many a summer morning when—
full of gratitude, full of joy—
you come into harbors seen for the first time;
may you stop at Phoenician trading centers
and buy fine things,
mother of pearl and coral, amber and ebony,
sensual perfumes of every kind.
as many sensual perfumes as you can;
may you visit numerous Egyptian cities
to fill yourself with learning from the wise.

Keep Ithaka always in mind.
Arriving there is what you're destined for.
But don't hurry the journey at all.
Better if it goes on for years
so you're old by the time you reach the island,
wealthy with all you've gained on the way,
not expecting Ithaka to make you rich.

Ithaka gave you the marvelous journey.
Without her you wouldn't have set out.
She hasn't anything else to give.

And if you find her poor, Ithaka won't have fooled
    you.
Wise as you'll have become, and so experienced,
you'll have understood by then what an Ithaka means.

> C. P. Cavafy, "Ithaka,"
> translated by Edmund Keeley
> and Philip Sherrard

IF I HAD MY LIFE TO LIVE OVER

I'd dare to make more mistakes next time. I'd relax, I would limber up. I would be sillier than I have been this trip. I would take fewer things seriously. I would take more chances. I would climb more mountains and swim more rivers. I would eat more ice cream and less beans. I would perhaps have more actual troubles, but I'd have fewer imaginary ones.

You see, I'm one of those people who live sensibly and

sanely hour after hour, day after day. Oh, I've had my moments, and if I had it to do over again, I'd have more of them. In fact, I'd try to have nothing else. Just moments, one after another, instead of living so many years ahead of each day. I've been one of those persons who never goes anywhere without a thermometer, a hot water bottle, a raincoat and a parachute. If I had to do it again, I would travel lighter than I have.

If I had my life to live over, I would start barefoot earlier in the spring and stay that way later in the fall. I would go to more dances. I would ride more merry-go-rounds. I would pick more daisies.

> Attributed to Nadine Stair,
> an eighty-five-year-old
> Kentucky woman

If I'd known how long I was going to live, I would have taken better care of myself.

> Attributed to Eubie Blake

INDEX BY NAMES

Asterisk suggests possible readings at a funeral service or memorial service

Index by Titles and Selected First Lines

Asterisk suggests possible readings at a funeral service or memorial service

NOTES